Philippine Myths, Legends, and Folktales

MAXIMO D. RAMOS

PHOENIX PUBLISHING HOUSE
927 Quezon Avenue, Quezon City

Reprinted 1998

Copyright 1990 by
Phoenix Publishing House, Inc.,
and Maximo D. Ramos

ALL RIGHTS RESERVED

No part of this book may be reproduced
in any form or by any means without
the prior written permission of the
author and the publisher.

Editorial Board

Editor	Estela Infante-Tan
Managing Editor	Victoria R. Tanjuatco
Art Director	David S. Cruz
Editorial Assistants	Raphael C. Cristobal
	Emiliano B. Guevara
Cover Design	Adriano L. Natividad

Illustration	Jonathan Panaguiton
Printer	Phoenix Press, Inc

JLLA MPI

MEMBER:
PHILIPPINE EDUCATIONAL
PUBLISHERS ASSOCIATION

Contents

Preface	vii
From the Publisher	ix

WHEN THE WORLD WAS YOUNG

How People Were Created	3
Why the Sun Is Brighter than the Moon	6
The Coleto and the Crow	9
The Legend of Mount Kanlaon	12
Why Dogs Bare Their Teeth	17
The Origin of Bananas	21

IN THE PHILIPPINE ELFLAND

The Two Woodcutters and the Elf	27
The Wee Folk	31
The Frog Princess	34
The Bridge of the Angels	39
Two Boys and a Tianak	42
The Elf's Gifts	47

TALES OF LAUGHTER

The Tale of Pakungo-adipen	56
The Man and the Lizard	61

The Man Who Played Dead	64
The Two Foolish Peddlers	68

ANIMALS AND PEOPLE

The Monkeys and the Butterflies	73
Three Friends Seek a Home	76
The Monkey Prince	80
Tale of the Kind-hearted Manobo	84
The Monkey Who Became a Servant	88

ADVENTURE TALES

Death and Datu Omar	96
The Man Who Reached the Sky-World	101
The Buried Treasure	105
The Tale of Magbaloto	108
Tale of the 101 Brothers and Their Sister	115
The Tale of Sog-sogot	126
The Enchanted Snail	132
The Man Who Tried to Cheat Death	136
The Tale of Diwata	140

Preface

THE FOLKLORE MATERIAL put together in this book is from all over the Philippines. Some are from the Ilocos region and the Cordilleras in the Christian and pagan north. Many are from the Christian provinces in the rest of Luzon and the Visayan Islands. The others are from Mindanao and the Sulu group in the pagan and Muslim South.

Represented here are the ethnic groups of the plains and coastal areas, of the foothills and mountains, of the swamps and rain forests. They were originally told in Bikol, Bontok, Ifugao, Iloko, Kalinga, Maranao, Pampango, Tagalog, Tausug, Tinguian, Visayan, and other Philippine vernaculars.

An attempt was made to exclude from this collection any material that showed borrowings from the West. But the attempt may not have fully succeeded, for in matters of folklore one cannot always tell what is Western and what is Eastern. The East and the West have been blending nicely in the Philippines ever since Magellan discovered the country for the white man in 1521. Moreover, most folklorists think that Asia, to which the Philippines geographically belongs, was the early home of many of folktales of Europe and America.

Folklore scholars define myths as narratives about the beginnings of the world, legends as narrative accounts of origins that occurred somewhat later than what happen in myths, and folktales as stories about the daily lives of the coomon folk of today or in the recent past.

It is hoped that the myths, legends, and folktales included in this book will help the reader get acquainted with the cultural past of the Philippines. And it is hoped that they will fire the reader's imagination as all good narratives, no matter where they originated, should do.

From The Publisher

MAXIMO D. RAMOS, the first editor in chief of Phoenix Publishing House, was associated with the company from 1963 until his death on December 12, 1988. As editor and consultant, he gathered together a team of teachers who were creative, understood the needs of Filipino students, knew their pedagogy, and, above all, were committed to the ideals of nationhood espoused by my father, Dr. Ernesto Y. Sibal.

The present leadership of Phoenix Publishing House in the textbook field in all subject areas on all three levels of the educational system is due, in a large measure, to the unfaltering loyalty and passion for work of Dr. Ramos.

Dr. Ramos never relaxed his own personal pursuit of the Muse and continued to write short stories, poems, and essays. At the same time, he devoted special attention to serious research on Philippine mythology and folklore. All these were done as he taught and performed administrative duties at the Philippine Normal College and later at the University of the East.

Phoenix Publishing House takes pride in publishing these ten volumes of the essential works of Dr. Ramos. We know that his legacy will fire the imagination of Filipino students and inspire them to know more about their own folkways and folklore and to write them down for others to enjoy and appreciate. Dr. Ramos's only limitation perhaps is access to Filipino language as medium of his literary output. But he has shown the Filipino student that one can master the English language and use it to advantage in portraying Philippine reality. And because the setting is Filipino and the experiences are part of the Filipino tradition, we know that his writings will appeal to children and to adults as well.

His works, collectively titled REALMS OF MYTHS AND REALITY, consist of the following:

    I. TALES OF LONG AGO IN THE PHILIPPINES
   II. PHILIPPINE MYTHS, LEGENDS, AND FOLKTALES
  III. LEGENDS OF LOWER GODS
  IV. THE CREATURES OF MIDNIGHT
   V. THE ASWANG COMPLEX IN PHILIPPINE FOLKLORE
  VI. PHILIPPINE DEMONOLOGICAL LEGENDS AND THEIR CULTURAL BEARINGS
 VII. BOYHOOD IN MONSOON COUNTRY
VIII. PATRICIA OF THE GREEN HILLS AND OTHER STORIES
  IX. REMEMBRANCE OF LENTS PAST AND OTHER ESSAYS
   X. THE CREATURES OF PHILIPPINE LOWER MYTHOLOGY

This collection is our tribute to Dr. Maximo D. Ramos and our contribution to Filipiniana.

J. ERNESTO SIBAL
Publisher

When the World Was Young

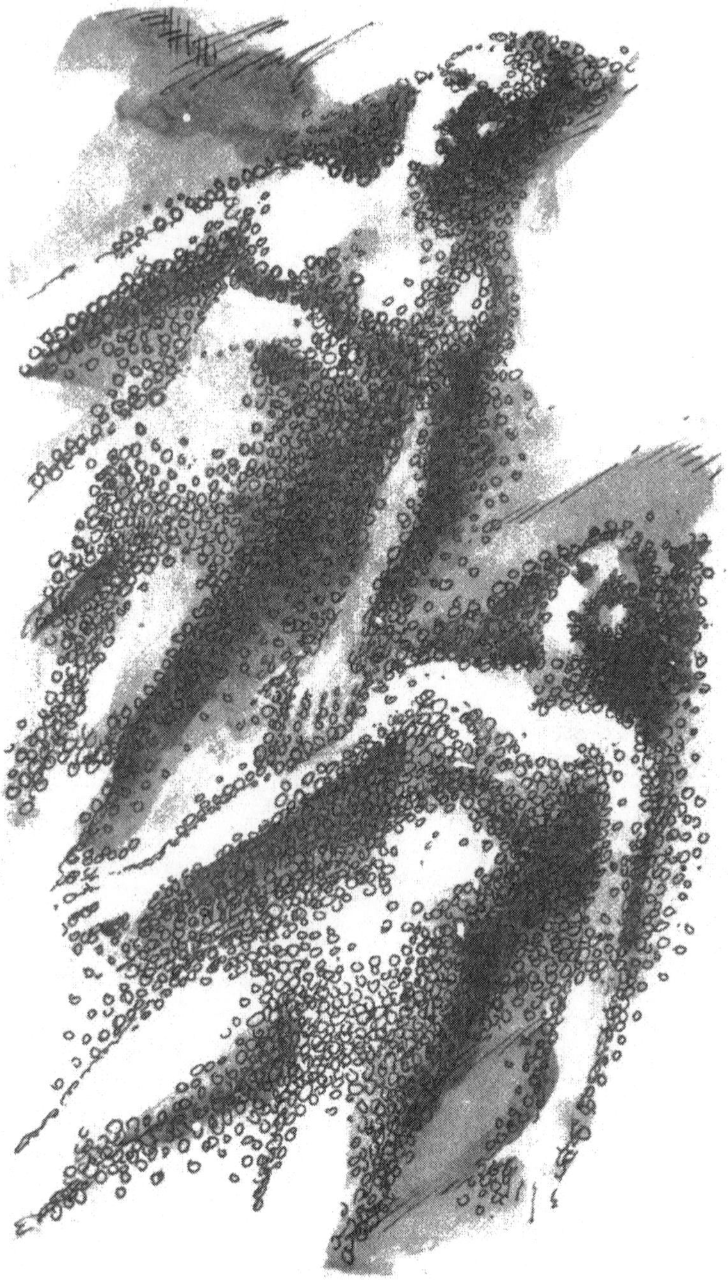

How People Were Created

A LONG TIME AGO, according to the Bagobos of Southern Mindanao, there was not a single man or woman in the whole wide world. There lived only Tuglay and Tuglibon, the two mighty beings who had created the world.

One day Tuglay spoke to Tuglibon and said: "Wife, perhaps it would be better if there were people in the world."

"It would be far better indeed," replied Tuglibon. "There should be people who will enjoy the beautiful new world we have made. Let us create a man and a woman who will love the blue sky and the wide sea. Let us create people who will love the flowers in the valleys and the clouds on the mountains."

So Tuglay took some corn meal in his hands, moistened it, and shaped it into human figures. Then he covered the figures with scales and gave them life.

When the creatures stood up, however, they looked very wooden, for Tuglay had forgotten to make joints in their bones. Their arms and legs were very stiff and they often stumbled to the ground when they walked. Moreover, their eyes were very small, their ears were half hidden, and their noses could hardly be seen. But worst of all, they could not hold anything with their stiff fingers, and because their bodies were covered with scales, they looked more like reptiles than human beings.

"I am not pleased with the people you made," said Tuglibon. "Better try again."

But Tuglay felt satisfied with them. "I think they will do," he said.

The more Tuglibon looked at them, however, the more she disliked them. "How will the world look when it's full of these ugly creatures?" she said. "I want people who can move about gracefully and who are not covered with scales as if they were serpents.".

"These two are good enough for me," Tuglay replied coldly. "I will not change them."

Tuglibon spoke no more about the matter, but she felt very uneasy thinking of the ill-shaped creatures. At last, when she could think of no better thing to do, she threw a handful of corn meal into her husband's eyes. "Now he will not see me work," she told herself.

Quickly she moistened the rest of the corn meal and shaped it into human figures. She made joints in their bones. She gave them bright eyes for seeing, well-shaped ears for hearing, larger noses for smelling, and pretty mouths for eating and speaking. She gave them smooth skins for feeling, putting scales only at the tips of their toes

and fingers. Finally, after she had given them each a big heart for loving, she put life into them. Then she made them stand up, and they were beautiful to look at.

When her work was finished, Tuglibon washed the corn meal out of Tuglay's eyes. Tuglay was very angry for what she had done to him, but upon seeing the man and woman, he was convinced that they were indeed better-looking than those he had made. "I am glad you made them," he said. "They and their children will be the rulers of the world."

"They will love only the beautiful and shun the ugly," Tuglibon said. "They will enjoy the songs of the birds, and they will wash their bodies in the cool springs and rivers. They will love each other, and watching the sun by day and the moon and stars by night, they will love us who created them."

So saying, Tuglay and Tuglibon smiled at the first man and woman who became the ancestors of the people now living on earth.

As for the scaly creatures that Tuglay made, nothing more was heard of them.

Why the Sun Is Brighter than the Moon

BATHALA, the creator of the world, had a son named Apolaki and a daughter named Mayari. The light that shone upon the world and enabled the people, the beasts, the birds, and the fish to see came from the bright eyes of Apolaki and Mayari. So all the creatures loved them dearly.

Bathala himself was very fond of his children, and he watched over them as they wandered across the meadows of heaven. Since the eyes of Apolaki and Mayari shone continuously, it was always day on the earth.

In time Bathala grew feeble with age and died. Then Apolaki and Mayari had a quarrel, for each wanted to rule the world alone. "I am the man and I will succeed my father to the throne," said Apolaki. "I am going to rule the world, whether you like it or not."

Mayari's eyes flashed with anger and she said, "I am no less my father's child than you. I will succeed him to his throne, whether you like it or not!"

The quarrel grew from bad to worse, and finally words could not express their furious rage. So they picked up wooden clubs and fell upon each other with fierce blows. Back and forth they fought until at last Apolaki struck Mayari in the face and she became blind in one eye.

When he saw his sister stricken, Apolaki took pity on her and said, "Let us fight no more, my sister. Let us share our father's kingdom equally between us. Let us reign by turns and be friends."

Mayari agreed, and from then on, Apolaki, whom we know today as the Sun, has ruled the world half the time. Mayari, whom we now know as the Moon, has taken turns with her brother in ruling the world. When Apolaki is on the throne, the world is flooded with warm light, because the light beams from his two bright eyes. On the other hand, when Mayari is reigning, the world is bathed with cool and gentle light, for she is blind in one eye.

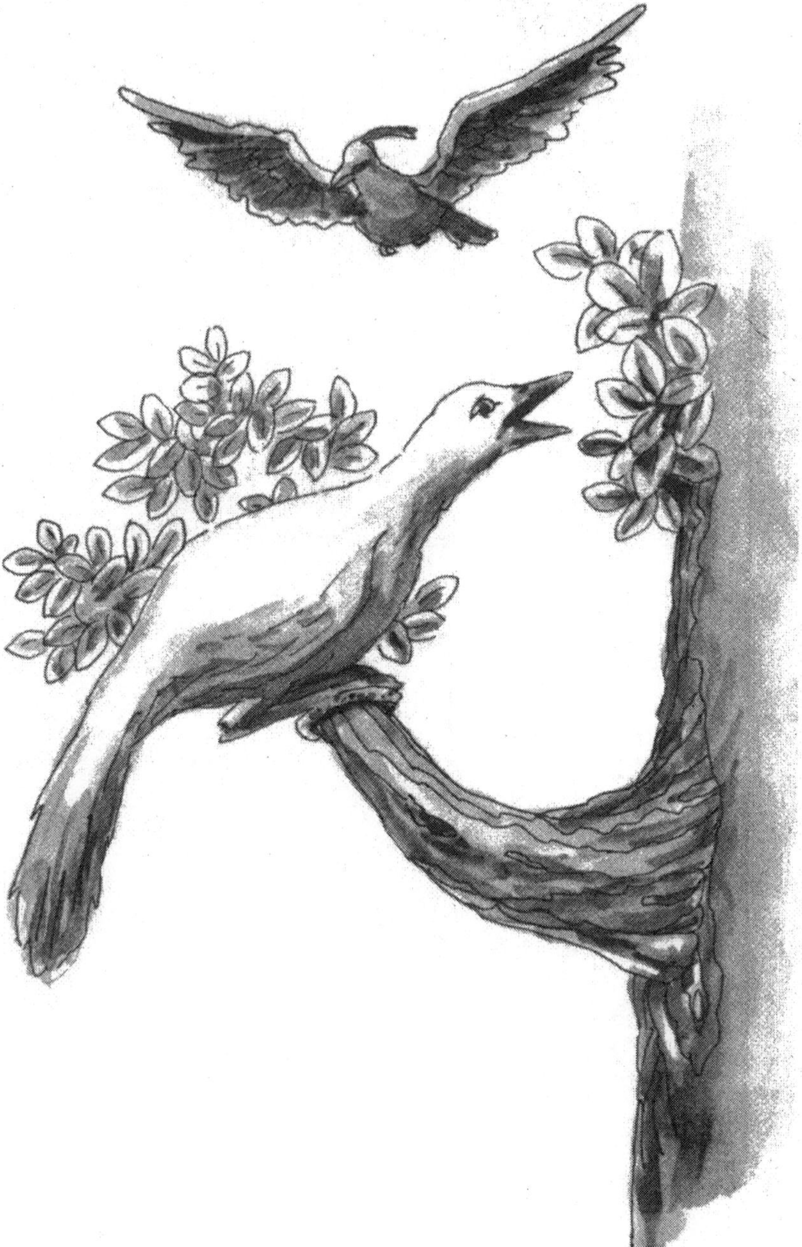

The Coleto and the Crow

IF YOU WANT TO KNOW why the crow is black and why the coleto has no feathers on top of his head, this Tagalog legend will tell you:

Once upon a time the crow was a white bird. The coleto, a bird as small as a maya, was as black as he is today, but he was not bald-headed then. There was a thick crest of feathers on top of his head.

One cool day the crow was up in a tree practicing his voice. "Wak! Wak! Wak!" he said.

Along came the coleto and said in his musical voice: "What a sweet song you have! I wish I were deaf. Then I would not hear your voice."

This remark annoyed the crow, for he knew that his voice was unpleasant and that he needed much singing practice. "If my voice is not sweet," said he, "neither am I as tiny as you are."

"It's true that I am tiny!" said the coleto, suddenly getting angry because he was very sensitive about his size. "Yet I can fly much higher than any other bird in the whole world. I can outfly the eagle himself."

"You must be mad to say that," said the crow. "How can you race the king of the birds? You cannot even race me."

The coleto laughed scornfully. "Would you like to have a test of wings with me?" said he. "Would you like to fly a race?"

"Better go home, Son," replied the crow. "Go home and eat more rice, drink more water, and breathe in more air. Wait till your wings are wider before you challenge me to a flying race."

"You forget that the smallest pepper is the hottest," said the coleto. "In the same way, a person's ability cannot be told by his size. You are no doubt bigger than I, but you are heavier and slower, too."

"If you want to fly a race, then let's fly a race and stop this talk," said the crow crossly. "Would you like the race to begin now?"

"Yes!"

The coleto counted three, and the race was on. Up and up, up and up they flew side by side, racing each other until they came to a dark cloud and lost sight of each other. So they flew on separately.

At last the coleto had flown so high that he knocked his head against the floor of the sky, and the skin on top of his head was scraped off. On the other hand, the crow flew so near the sun that his white feathers were burned.

They were both very much frightened by the experience, and when they returned to earth they forgot all about the race. But down to this day the coleto has no feathers on top of his head, and the crow's feathers are completely black.

The Legend of Mount Kanlaon

THE WIDE VALLEYS of Negros have always been green with cane fields tilled by a happy people. But once, in the olden days, there appeared a frightful dragon on the highest mountain in the island. The monster had seven ugly heads, and its dark green body was a full kilometer long. It snorted out hot smoke from its fourteen nostrils. From its seven cavernous mouths it belched torrents of death-dealing fire.

The smoke from its nostrils and the fire from its mouths ruined the crops in the fields, burned down whole towns, and killed hundreds of men, women, and children. So the people were in constant dread of the dragon. They sought all sorts of ways to appease it, but its wrath did not abate.

At last it was found that if a beautiful maiden was offered to the dragon, it would not molest the people for a whole year. So at the beginning of each year the priests chose the fairest maiden in the kingdom. They dressed her in a black robe and took her to the slopes of the mountain. There a religious ceremony followed and then she was left alone on the mountain. She was never heard of again, but the people knew that the dragon had devoured her, and for twelve moons no fire or smoke would descend upon the valleys.

This went on year after year. But soon no maiden

could be found beautiful enough to be acceptable to the dragon. Every father had learned to make ugly marks on the face of his daughter when she was still a baby. In this way he would not run the risk of losing her when she grew up into a young woman.

At last only the king's daughter remained. She was beautiful beyond words. No one had had the heart to mutilate her lovely face. All felt sure she would become queen after her father's death, and of course the people knew that to be ruled by a queen with an ugly face would be hard indeed.

The priests sought everywhere for another maiden whom the dragon might accept as a sacrifice, but all the virgins they found had ugly faces.

"What shall we do?" the king asked, raising his hands in despair. Ominous bursts of smoke and fierce tongues of flame had begun to appear at the top of the dragon's mountain.

"Indeed, what shall we do?" asked the people.

Nothing else could be done, so it was at last decided to sacrifice the king's daughter rather than feel the dragon's wrath again.

Just then there appeared in the kingdom a handsome young stranger attired in the robes of a great prince from

India. He walked to the palace, stood before the king, and said:

"I heard about your troubles and have come to see what I can do to help."

"Thank you indeed," said the king. "Slay the dragon or even just drive it away and you shall be rewarded with all the gold you can carry, and my daughter shall be yours."

The stranger left without another word. He climbed up the slopes of the mountain and saw ants crawling on the ground, bees sipping nectar from the flowers, and eagles soaring among the clouds high up overhead.

Now the stranger was really the great god Laon. He was skilled in talking with the birds, the beasts, and the insects in their own language. He now spoke to one of the ants and said:

"I am your Lord Laon. Hurry to your king and tell him it is my command that he march with all his warriors to the top of this mountain. He must help fight the dragon."

"Yes, Khan Laon," replied the ant and scurried off with a courteous bow.

Likewise the great god Laon spoke to one of the bees

14

and said: "I am your Lord Laon. Fly to your king and tell him it is my command that he bring all the bees to the top of the mountain. He must help fight the dragon."

"Yes, Khan Laon," replied the bee with a courteous bow and buzzed away.

Then the great god Laon beckoned to one of the eagles circling high up in the clouds. It swooped down, stood before the god, and said, "What does my Lord Laon command me to do?"

"Fly to your king and tell him it is my command that he bring all the eagles to the top of this mountain. He must help fight the dragon."

"Yes, Khan Laon," replied the eagle and whizzed off with a courteous bow.

When they heard the command of the great god Laon, the king of the ants, the king of the bees, and the king of the eagles gathered all their followers and advanced to the top of the mountain. The ants crawled as fast as they could and the bees and eagles shot through the air at great speed.

Meanwhile Laon had an eagle fly with him to the top of the mountain. There he saw the dragon's immense body sprawled over the rocks and crags. With its fierce green eyes the monster saw him and began snorting out hot smoke from its fourteen nostrils and belching deadly fire from its seven mouths.

Then the people in the valleys grew alarmed and began to blame the king. "The stranger has aroused the dragon's wrath!" said they. "Why did our king allow him to wake up the sleeping monster?"

The king himself sat worried on his throne. And the princess, who had seen the stranger when he first arrived and had fallen in love with him, fretted in her chamber. "He will get killed, he will get killed!" she moaned to herself.

Then the large army of ants—red ants, black ants, blue ants, brown ants—swarmed all over the dragon's body. They crept under its great scales and bit the dragon with all their might.

At the same time the bees—carpenter bees and honey bees and bumble bees—flew in and stung the fierce green eyes of the dragon until the monster was completely blind.

The dragon snorted more smoke out of its nostrils and belched more deadly fire from its seven mouths. At the same time its fearful claws stabbed the air and its vast body coiled and uncoiled on the rocks and boulders.

Then the eagles swooped in like feathered lightnings and pecked out the monster's fourteen eyes.

At last the great god Laon drew his flashing sword and faced the dragon. The dragon threw out clouds of stifling smoke and floods of fire. It slashed the air blindly with its terrible claws. But the great god chopped off its heads one by one. When its largest and ugliest head was finally cut off, the dragon grew still and died.

The great god Laon bore the dragon's largest head on his shoulder and returned to the valley. There he was met by the people with great rejoicing. But happiest of all those who met him was the king's lovely daughter. She and Laon were married, needless to say, and they became the ancestors of the present good people of Negros.

For the god's great exploit, the people named the dragon's mountain Khan Laon, or Lord Laon, after him. But among us of today, who want to say things in a great hurry, "Khan Laon" has become "Kanlaon."

Why Dogs Bare Their Teeth

ONCE THERE LIVED a rich man who had two pets, a dog and a cat. The dog was old and had lost all his teeth, but he knew all the paths in the town. The cat was still young, but she could not run long errands because she did not know the way. She was afraid to wander far from her master's house.

One day the man said to his pets, "You two, go to the next town and give this ring to my daughter. You cat," he added, "because you are very careful about things you carry, I shall let you hold the ring. And you dog, show the cat which way to go, and do not let anyone steal the ring."

The cat and the dog promised to do as they were told, and they set out on their journey.

Now a swift river lay in their path. There was no bridge across the river and so they tried to look for a boat. They found no boat, however, but they did not give up their journey, for in those days cats loved to swim as much as dogs and people did, although to be sure cats could not swim so well.

Now the dog became worried about the ring. As they were about to cross the river, he turned to the cat and said, "Let me hold the ring while we are in the water. I am afraid you will drop the ring."

"No, no!" replied the cat. "Our master told me to hold the ring. I will not give you the ring."

"Better give it to me," the dog insisted. "I am sure I can hold it better than you."

"I will not give you the ring!" repeated the cat, her eyes glowing with wrath.

The dog grew angry, too, and said, "Will you give me the ring or not?" He approached the cat and prepared to take the ring by force.

The cat was frightened and gave the ring to him. "If you lose it, I am not to blame," she said.

Then they started to swim across. The river was so swift that they soon grew tired. The cat began to be carried downstream and was about to turn back when she heard a piercing cry of grief. "I have lost the ring!" wailed the dog. "The river has carried it off. What shall I do?" He looked very much worried.

"See what I told you?" said the cat. "Let us go back and tell our master."

"I'll stay and look for the ring," said the dog, and he began diving into the water.

But though he tried very hard, he never found the ring. At last he turned back and followed the cat homeward.

He had gone halfway when he was overcome with fear and ran into the woods to hide.

"I did not expect you so soon," said the master when the cat came back. "Did you give the ring to my daughter?"

The cat shook her head.

Seeing that the cat was alone, the man asked, "Where is the dog?"

"He ran away, Master," said the cat. "He — he lost the ring."

"He lost the ring!" the master shouted. "I told you not to give him the ring!"

Then the cat told him what had happened, and when the master heard her story, he was very angry indeed. "I must punish that dog!" he shouted.

So he called all the other dogs in the town and told them to hunt for the culprit. "Bring him back and I will give you much gold," said he. I do not know why he promised them gold, which dogs never use, instead of bones, which all dogs love. But gold the master promised them, and they seemed very much interested in earning it.

"How can we tell him from the other dogs, Master?" they asked.

"He has no teeth," replied the man. "Bring him back, and his tail shall be cut off."

So the dogs went in search of the missing culprit. They hunted this way and that way and the other way, but they never found him.

They never gave up hunting, however, and down to our own day the dogs and their puppies all over the world have been hunting for the dog who lost the ring. Whenever one dog meets another, each one asks, "Are you he who lost my master's ring?"

To that question they all give an emphatic "No" by shaking their tails. And they try to prove that they are not the culprit by baring their teeth. "Look, I have complete teeth!" they say. "He who lost the ring was toothless."

And so the search continues to this day. The baring of teeth and the wagging of tails has never stopped, for you see they are still looking for the toothless dog who lost the ring.

Meanwhile, the cat was so frightened by her experience in the water that she has never dared swim again.

The Origin of Bananas

WOULD YOU LIKE to know how bananas came into the world? Then stop pulling one another's hair and I shall tell you.

Once, in Lanao, there was a kingdom of green fields, clear streams, and blue hills. A princess ruled the beautiful kingdom, and she was so kind, so beautiful, and so wise that her subjects did everything they could to make her happy.

"Let us raise enough food in our fields," said the men. "Then our queen will be happy."

"Let us keep our towns clean and our homes neat," said the women. "Then our queen will feel proud of us all."

"Let us be obedient and good," said the children. "Then the queen and our parents will always love us."

And you may not believe it but what they promised to do they did. The men burned down the cockpits and gambling houses and worked on their farms all day. The women kept their homes as clean and shiny as your uncle's bald head. And the children became so good that their parents threw away their whips and their teachers thought less of how to make them learn their lessons and more of what lessons to teach them.

But one person in the kingdom was not at all happy. She was a wicked cousin of the queen's. She wanted to rule in place of the queen and thought of ways to rob the queen of her throne.

The years went by and the queen ruled alone. From many foreign lands kings and princes came begging her for her love. But the queen said: "If I take one of you the others will be angry. Then there will be war. I would rather remain single and have peace in my kingdom than take a husband and cause trouble."

Now the wicked cousin of the queen's secretly loved one of the suitors. She thought of a plan and took this suitor aside. Then she whispered in his ear: "Why do you waste time? My cousin the queen loves you. But she cannot accept your love because she is afraid that if she does, the other suitors will make war on her kingdom. Bring your army here, therefore, and slay your rivals and the queen's guards. Then enter the city, and the queen and her kingdom will be yours."

The suitor believed her and left for his native land. Then he gathered his ablest soldiers and hurried back to the queen's realm.

In the meantime, a brightly colored magic bird, the Nori, had heard the wicked woman plotting with the suitor. The Nori flew to the queen's window, fluttered its wings, and said, "Listen, O queen! I wish to speak with you."

"Speak on," replied the queen.

"Know that one of your suitors plans to kill his rivals and your guards. He plans to take you by force and marry you. But that is not the end of the matter. Your cousin wants your crown and will not rest until she has slain you and won your husband's love."

Having spoken, the magic bird flew away, and the queen was greatly troubled. "Alas," she sighed, "I have tried to rule my kingdom wisely and well. I have tried to please my people the best way I can. But my own cousin wants to betray me!"

Her heart was heavy with sorrow. She wept bitterly as though her heart would break, but she showed her grief to no one.

When night came she asked everyone in the palace—the servants, the courtiers, and the guards—to go outside the palace walls. The people wondered why the queen made such a strange request, but they thought she must have good reasons because she had never done anything unwise before.

When they were gone, the queen locked up herself in her chamber and set the room on fire. The fire quickly spread into the other rooms. The people saw the flames and tried to rush in to put out the fire. But the queen had locked the palace gates, too, and with the entire palace she perished in the flames.

The people mourned deeply over the death of their queen and built a beautiful fence around her ashes. "We must honor her who loved us so well," they said.

One morning, not long after, a strange plant appeared on the pile of ashes. It had long, wide leaves and a straight white trunk. There were no thorns on the trunk of the tree, and it fluttered its leaves gracefully in the wind.

The plant came to be known as the banana. "It is our queen," said the people to one another. "She has come to life again."

The banana plant grew, and in time a red, heart-shaped flower came out of its bosom. Slender fruit came from the flower. The fruit ripened, and the people, tasting it, said:

"It is delicious! It is our queen's gift to us!"

So they ate the fruit, and all agreed that their queen's gift was as sweet as she had always been.

As for the queen's wicked cousin, God turned her into a monkey. She found the queen's gift very delicious and she has liked the banana more than any other fruit.

In the Philippine Elfland

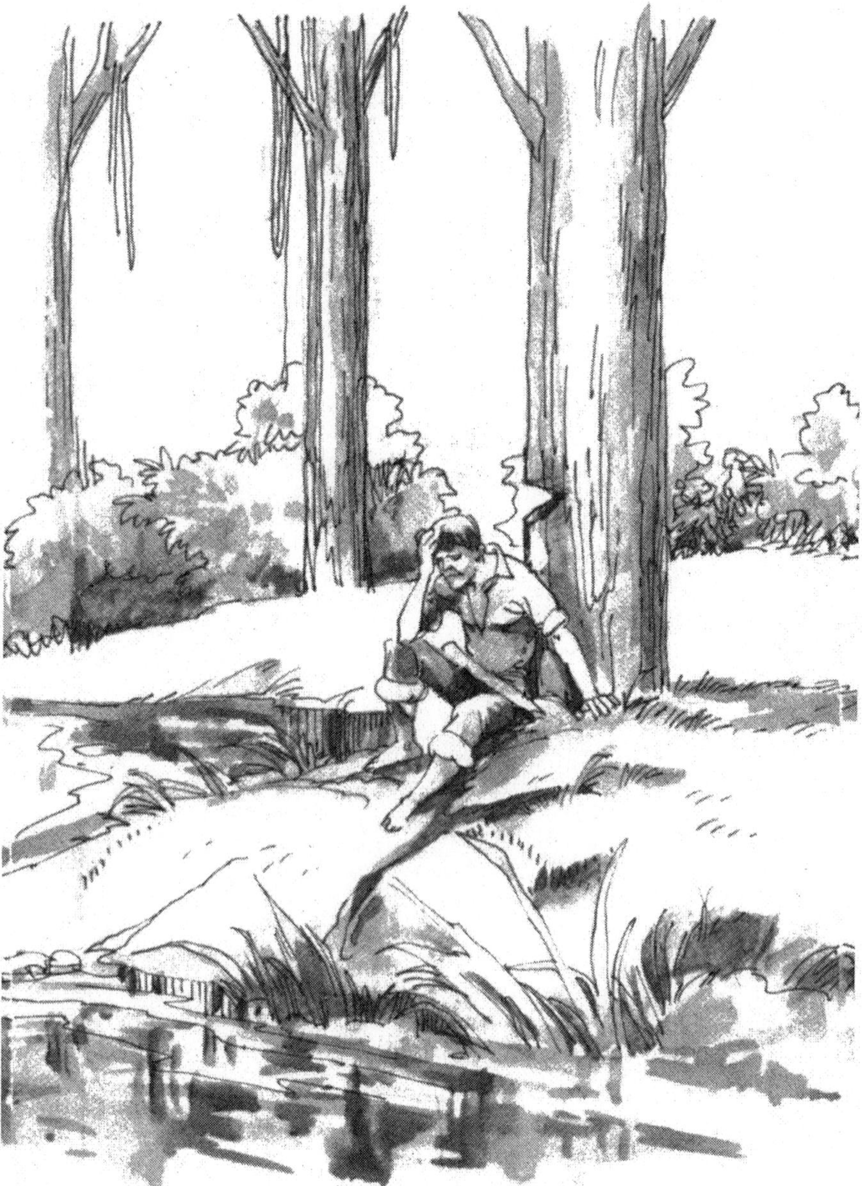

The Two Woodcutters and the Elf

ONE AFTERNOON a poor woodcutter entered the forest to chop down a tree for firewood. He chose a tall, straight tree beside a dark lake and started swinging his axe. The ring of the axe echoed and reechoed through the wilderness.

The woodcutter worked fast, for he hoped to finish cutting down the tree before nightfall. But the blade of his axe became loose, slipped off the handle, and fell into the lake.

The man dived into the water to find the blade, but though he dived again and again, he failed to find it. The woodcutter sat at the foot of the tree wondering what he should do, when suddenly an elf appeared before him and asked:

"What is troubling you, good man?"

"The blade of my axe fell into the water," he replied. "I wonder how I can get it."

"Let me see what I can do," said the elf, diving into the lake.

Soon she broke the surface holding an axe blade of pure gold. It shone brightly in the sun as the water dripped from it. "Is this your axe blade?" she asked.

As I said before, the woodcutter was a poor man. He knew that if he could have the gold blade he would be the richest man in the barrio. But he promptly shook his head at the question and said, "No, that's not mine."

The elf left the blade on the bank and dived in again.

By and by she emerged from the water holding an axe blade of shining silver. "Is this it?" she asked.

Again the woodcutter thought how much money he would get for the silver blade. But he shook his head as before and said, "No, that's not mine."

The elf left the blade beside the first one and dived in again.

Soon she reappeared on the surface, and this time she held the woodcutter's old iron blade. "Is this it?" she asked.

"Yes, that's my blade!" replied he. "Thank you very much for taking the trouble to find it!"

The elf gave the blade to him, but when the man started for home, she picked up the silver blade and the gold blade and said, "I admire you very much for your honesty. Because of this I should like to give you both the silver blade and the gold blade as a present."

The woodcutter thanked her again, took her gifts, and walked home happily.

Now the woodcutter had a neighbor, and when this neighbor saw the axe blades of silver and gold, he asked: "Where did you get them?"

"I was cutting a tree beside a lake in the woods," the other replied, "when the blade of my axe slipped off and fell into the water. I could not find it, and an elf came. She not only found the blade for me but she gave me these two as well." The woodcutter said nothing else, for he was not a man of many words.

"Tell me how to get there," said the other. "I want to go and try my luck, too."

The woodcutter told him how to find the way to the lake. Then the other hurried home, took his old axe, loosened the blade on its handle a little, and ran off into the woods.

He looked this way and that, walking deeper and deeper into the forest, until he found the lake. He saw the tree partly cut at the bank of the water and knew this was the place. So he started swinging his axe and his blows echoed and reechoed in the woods.

It did not take long before his loose axe blade slipped off and fell into the water. He dived in once, pretending to look for it. Then he sat at the bank of the lake, putting on a very sad face and pretending to cry over his misfortune.

By and by the elf appeared before him and said, "My good man, what are you so sad about?"

"I lost my dearest possession," replied he, moaning louder than before.

"What did you lose, and how did you lose it?"

"I was cutting down this tree," he replied, "when the blade of my axe slipped off and fell into the water. Then I put another blade on the handle and continued working. The second blade slipped off, too, and though I have dived so hard to find them, they are nowhere to be found." Then the man resumed his moaning.

"Stop weeping, old man," said the elf, "and I shall see what I can do." So saying, she dived into the water.

The man did not have to wait long. Soon the elf came out of the water holding up an axe blade of pure silver which shone in the afternoon sun.

"Is this the blade?" she asked.

The man took the blade from her and said, "Why, yes! That is my own silver blade! Thank you for finding it. Now there is only one more blade for me to find."

"I shall try to find it, too," said the elf and dived in again.

"Now," thought the man, "I shall be as rich as my neighbor."

After a few moments the elf emerged from the water holding an axe blade of shining gold. She held it before him and asked, "Is this the other blade?"

The man held out his hand to reach for it and said, "Yes, yes! This indeed is my second axe blade! What a good diver you are! Thank you for helping me."

But the elf held the blade off from him and said, "You shall have neither of these two blades. I only help those who are honest. Get out of my woods quickly or you will be sorry!" So saying, the elf took the silver blade from him, too, and disappeared.

The man felt very much ashamed and walked home. "Now I do not even have my old iron blade," he said to himself, and he wished he had been more honest.

The Wee Folk

THE OLD WOMAN finished winnowing rice under the bamboo tree just as the sun set. She piled up the chaff in a mound as high as an anthill and built a slow fire with the chaff. Then she went into her garden and dug up some yams, and she put the yams in the slow fire.

"When I wake up tomorrow morning," she told herself, "the yams will be just right for breakfast."

She went into her hut and cooked supper, and then she ate and went to bed.

The cocks had not been crowing long early the next morning before she hurried down her ladder to take the yams out of the fire. "I shall have a delicious breakfast of roasted yams," she said.

But whichever part of the fire she looked, not a single yam did she find. "Ah, the *kiba-an* have been in my yard!" she said.

Now, by *kiba-an* the old woman meant the unseen wee folk who delight in such petty mischiefs as stealing rice from the housewife's bin, running off with the fish in the fisherman's traps, or pulling off hair from children's heads. The kiba-an's skin is as light as the skin of the white man, and its mouth shines with its gold teeth. Another queer thing about the kiba-an is that its heels point before and its toes behind, misleading people who follow its footprints. The kiba-an's long hair reaches down to its feet, and some people say they have often seen groups of them singing on vines in the bamboo groves or dancing in the woods to the music of wee, wee guitars. Sometimes, in the night, the wee folk wander into people's yards, and so, when throwing things out of their windows, people say, "Get out of the way!" For if by mistake people should hurt them, the kiba-an will give them sickness or cause their death.

Well, the next day after sundown the old woman built another mound of chaff, kindled it, and put more yams in the fire. Then she cooked supper and ate. But after supper, instead of going to bed, she sat down to listen at the window.

In a trice she heard tiny voices saying: "Aha-ha-hai! The old woman's yams — how nice they taste!"

"It is just as I thought!" the old woman told herself. "The kiba-an are eating the yams."

She went to bed, and the next morning she walked to the mound of burning chaff and found that the yams were gone again. "It was the kiba-an, all right," she said.

So when the sun set once more, she built another

mound of rice chaff and kindled it. But she did not go into the garden to dig up more yams. Instead she walked to the river and chose a few stones as big as her fists, and then she walked home and put the stones in the fire.

She sat listening at her window after supper, and very soon she heard the same wee voices. But this time there was no laughter in those voices. "Na-ai-i-i!" one of the wee folk said. "I thought these were yams!"

"I, too, thought these were yams!" said another.

"But these are only stones!" added a third.

"These are only hard stones!" said the others.

Soon the wee voices faded into the night, and all was still.

Came another sunset, and the old woman built a new fire under the bamboo. In the fire she placed yams once more, and next morning the roasted yams were all there and just right for breakfast.

"It will be some time before the wee folk come into my yard again," said the old woman to herself with a little laugh.

The Frog Princess

THE OLD KING was dying. So to his bedside he called his three sons, Diego, Pedro, and Juan. "You each go and look for your wives," he said. "I should like to see the three of you married before I die."

"Yes, Father," they replied and got set to go and seek for their wives.

As they were leaving, the king added, "Go your separate ways, knock at the door of the first house you come to, and whoever opens the door, ask her to marry you."

The three princes agreed to do what their father told them. Then they mounted their strong horses and galloped away.

The road soon forked. They set a day on which they should all return and agreed to meet at the same spot so that they could go home together. Then they went their separate ways.

After many weary days of travel, Diego, the eldest of the three, came to a large palace. He knocked at the door and a beautiful princess opened it. She was so slender that Diego could have encircled her waist with his thumb and middle finger. She agreed to marry him and went along with him.

Pedro, who was next to Diego in years, likewise came to a great palace and tapped at the door. Out came a lovely princess whose skin was so fine and clear that the water could be seen trickling down her throat when she drank. The princess agreed to become Pedro's wife and went along with him.

Juan, the youngest, came to a tiny hut and knocked at the door. It opened, and out jumped an ugly frog. "Gak!"

the frog croaked at Juan. Its voice was hoarse and its skin slimy, but Juan knelt down and picked it up tenderly.

"Dear frog," he said, "I have come a long way looking for you. Will you marry me?"

"Gak!" the frog replied.

Juan took that to mean yes, so he put the frog in his hat and headed for home.

The three brothers met at the time and place they had agreed on. Proudly Diego and Pedro boasted about the princesses they had found and won. They laughed when, asking Juan whom he had brought home for a wife, he showed them the ugly frog.

The king met them and was pleased with the two princesses. But he almost went out of his wits with rage when Juan presented him with the frog. "Throw that creature out of the window!" he told Juan. "A frog for my daughter-in-law? Never!"

"But Father," said Juan, "you told us to return with whoever opened the door of the house we first entered. I knocked at the door of a tiny hut and this frog opened it. So I have brought her home."

"I said I will have no frog for a daughter-in-law!" repeated the king.

But Juan insisted that he loved the frog dearly, and so the king said no more about the matter.

The wedding day approached and the king ordered a great feast prepared. Criers hurried to all parts of the kingdom telling the people to join the feast.

A few days before the wedding the king said: "Let the brides weave their own veils."

The two princesses sat down to weave their veils, and the frog sat down to weave hers.

Diego's bride worked very hard, but the threads of the veil she made were not straight and the veil itself was out of shape.

Pedro's bride wove a coarse veil, and it was covered with betel stains.

The frog leaped over the skein and made an exquisite veil with flowers so dainty that you could almost smell their sweet garden fragrance.

At last came the great wedding day. Diego and Pedro were radiant with smiles as their brides leaned on their arms. For his part, Juan held the slimy green frog in his hand, and the people could hardly keep from laughing at him. The king was furious, but Juan insisted that he loved the frog and wanted to marry her.

Just as the veils were about to be thrown over the couples, the frog whispered, "Juan, please crush me under your foot."

Juan was very much pleased to hear the frog speak human words, but he did not want to do what it told him. "I do not want to kill you," he replied. "I want to marry you."

"Juan, please do what I told you," begged the frog. "Crush me under your foot." And so earnestly did she say it that finally Juan crushed the frog under his foot.

Then a wonderful thing happened. Where the frog had been there stood a princess so beautiful that the two other princesses appeared like servants beside her.

Of course everyone was delighted to see this happy turn of events. Everybody urged the frog-princess to tell her story and so she explained:

"I was a princess loved by my parents and my people. But a witch cast a spell over me. She turned me into a frog and said that only the love of a prince could break the spell. Long I waited for the prince to come along, and at last Juan came. Juan has given me his love, and so I have become my real self again."

Of the three couples, the king came to love Juan and the frog-princess best. So before he died he left the throne to his youngest son.

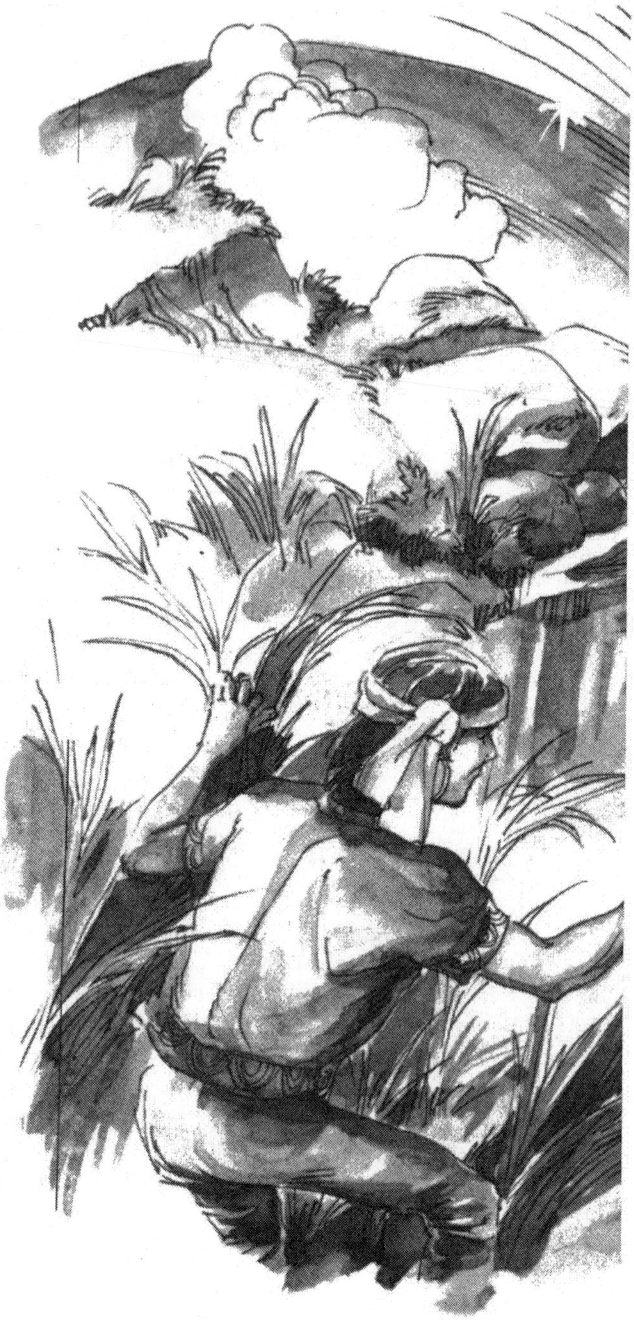

The Bridge of the Angels

ONE DAY a young datu was standing on a mountainside. The sun shone over the valley, and he looked up to behold a rainbow forming in the sky. He saw one end of the rainbow bend toward the mountain on which he stood admiring its perfect shape and its bright colors.

Then he remembered an old story he once heard about the rainbow. A white-haired old man had said that the rainbow was the bridge which the angels took whenever they came down to earth. "That is why one foot of the rainbow often rests on the side of a mountain," the man had said, adding: "Now if you run fast and get to the foot of the rainbow quick enough, you will find a fragrant pool there. Hide yourself and watch quietly, and you will see the angels — the *birad-dali* — come down to bathe in the pool."

The young datu watched the foot of the rainbow bend lower and lower. Soon it almost touched the tops of the trees that stood in a line winding down the mountainside. Then the rainbow swung away beyond the trees, and its foot descended further until it rested in a cogon patch well within running distance from where he stood.

Quite out of breath with excitement, he sprinted to the foot of the rainbow. Over rocks he ran, past a line of trees, and across the cogon grass.

Then he stopped and hid in the tall grass, for there, right at the foot of the rainbow, lay a mountain pool. The pool was clear and still, and on its margin were water lilies in bloom. The pool reflected the rainbow in all its glorious colors. There was a fragrance in the air, too, and inhaling this way and that, he found that the sweet odor came from the pool. "Everything the old man said is true!" he thought, watching from his hiding place in the grass.

More wonders followed, for looking up, he saw a beautiful angel come walking lightly down the rainbow. She resembled a princess of storyland coming down a palace stairway. She cast her glance here and there, and the young man could see that she was trying to make sure nobody was around.

But as I said before, he sat hidden in the tall grass, so the angel did not see him. Gracefully she alighted from the rainbow, her white feet twinkling above the water for a moment, and then she descended into the pool.

"How beautiful she is!" thought he. "I must go and speak to her." He came out of hiding, crept through the reeds, and then, when near enough, leapt into the water after her.

The angel was frightened, and with a splash she fled to the foot of the rainbow. But he caught her wrists in his hands and held her firmly before she could climb out of the water.

"Let me go! Let me go!" cried the angel, struggling to free herself.

"No, you must not go," he replied, and he held her more firmly still.

"Please let me go!" wailed the angel. "Let me go!"

"If you return to heaven," said he, "I can never hope to see you again. You must come home with me and be my bride."

"I have promised to marry a hero," sobbed the angel. "He died in a great battle of men only yesterday. I must go back to heaven. Let me go!"

"No, you must remain on earth with me," said he firmly.

Again the angel struggled to get free but he held her in his arms. "Oh, what shall I do!" she moaned.

"Life on earth is happy and interesting if one knows how to make it so," he told her. "If you agree to be my wife and live with me, you will become a mortal. But I will make you the happiest of mortals in all the world."

The angel was finally persuaded and he took her home with him.

When the people saw her, "How charming she is!" they all exclaimed. "Where did you find such a lovely princess?"

He told them his story, and the people wondered at her beauty all the more.

There followed a very merry wedding feast for her and the young datu, and after that, you may be sure they lived happily and virtuously all their earthly lives.

As to what happened after they died, I am sorry I cannot say, and the old men of Sulu who tell this story cannot say either. But since they lived so happily and so virtuously, I have no doubt that they went to heaven, where together they must have continued living their sweet and virtuous lives forever.

Two Boys and a Tianak

ONE DAY two friends, Yoyong and Mente, were walking through a coconut grove. Night was falling and the countryside was growing dark. When their path led them near some low-hanging trees, they heard a baby's cry.

"What's that?" Yoyong whispered.

"It's nothing," replied Mente. "Just a baby in its mother's arms. Maybe she is going home through the grove."

Then they heard the baby's cry again. It came from under the trees. The two friends stopped and looked at each other in silence.

"I wonder what a mother and her baby could be doing here so late in the day?" said Mente. "Let's find out."

"There are no people living here, and it's getting dark," said Yoyong. It was a cool evening but his face and neck were moist with sweat.

"You, a big boy, afraid of an infant!" laughed Mente. "Come, let's look for the baby."

Mente pulled Yoyong toward the trees. They walked to where the cries had come from, and soon under a big tree they saw a baby. He was kicking about and crying on a banana leaf spread on the ground.

"Poor baby!" said Mente, picking it up and kissing its cheeks. "It is cold!"

"And it must be hungry besides!" said Yoyong. "Where could its mother be?"

"I don't believe it has a mother," said Mente. "I'll take it home and raise it. When it grows big and I'm a man it will be my servant. It will cook my meals and serve me at the table and wash the dishes."

"No, you give me that baby," said Yoyong. "It's mine. I heard its cry first."

"It's mine!" replied Mente. "You may have heard it first, but you were for running away. You would have run away, too, if I did not force you to come with me and look for it."

Yoyong claimed the baby but Mente said the baby was his, and they grew angry with each other. Yoyong ran off to a bamboo fence and pulled out a stake to strike Mente with. Mente saw him and, putting down the baby, prepared to fight Yoyong.

But no sooner had he put the baby on the ground than a strange thing happened. In a twinkling the baby became an old man with an ugly, frightful face. He had a beard that hung down to his chest, and his face was covered with thick hair. His eyes were bright and small, and one of his legs was much longer than the other. He was a *tianak*.

When Mente saw the tianak, he became so terrified

that he turned to run away. But the tianak leaped after him and buried his sharp teeth in his arm. Mente screamed for help and when Yoyong heard him and saw the tianak, he became very much frightened, too. So he started running away and exclaiming: *"Susmariosep! Susmariosep!"*

No sooner were the words out of Yoyong's mouth than the tianak let go of Mente and vanished into the darkness.

Then Yoyong and Mente forgot their anger and ran away as fast as ever you please.

They reached home tired and breathing hard. Aling Nenang, Yoyong's mother, put some medicine where the tianak had bitten Mente.

"It's lucky that Yoyong said 'Susmariosep,'" Aling Nenang said. "Only that word can drive the tianak away."

"Please tell us more about the tianak," said Mente.

"The tianak looks frightful," she said. "But he does not harm you unless you harm him first or unless he sees you are afraid. Remember that when you see another tianak."

"I hope I will never see a tianak again," said Yoyong.

"Why does the tianak turn himself into a baby, Aling Nenang?" asked Mente.

"So that you will go near him," she replied. "When you are near enough, he changes himself into his ugly form to frighten you with his fearful looks. Then, if you become afraid, he will bite you."

"Does the tianak eat people?" Yoyong asked.

"No," she replied. "The tianak likes to frighten people, but I have never heard of anyone killed by a tianak."

"We saw another strange thing about the tianak," said Mente. "His legs."

"Was one leg much longer than the other?" she asked.

"Yes."

"Well, the tianak's right leg is always longer than his left," said Aling Nenang. "It is so long that when he squats on the ground, his right knee is far above his head but his left knee reaches only up to his chest."

"I don't think the tianak would be much of a runner then," said Yoyong. "One of his legs is too short. If he tries to run he will stumble."

"He is not much of a runner, to be sure," admitted Aling Nenang. "But he can leap far. He can leap very much farther than a man can. I tell you, boys," she added, "you better keep away from the tianak if you can help it."

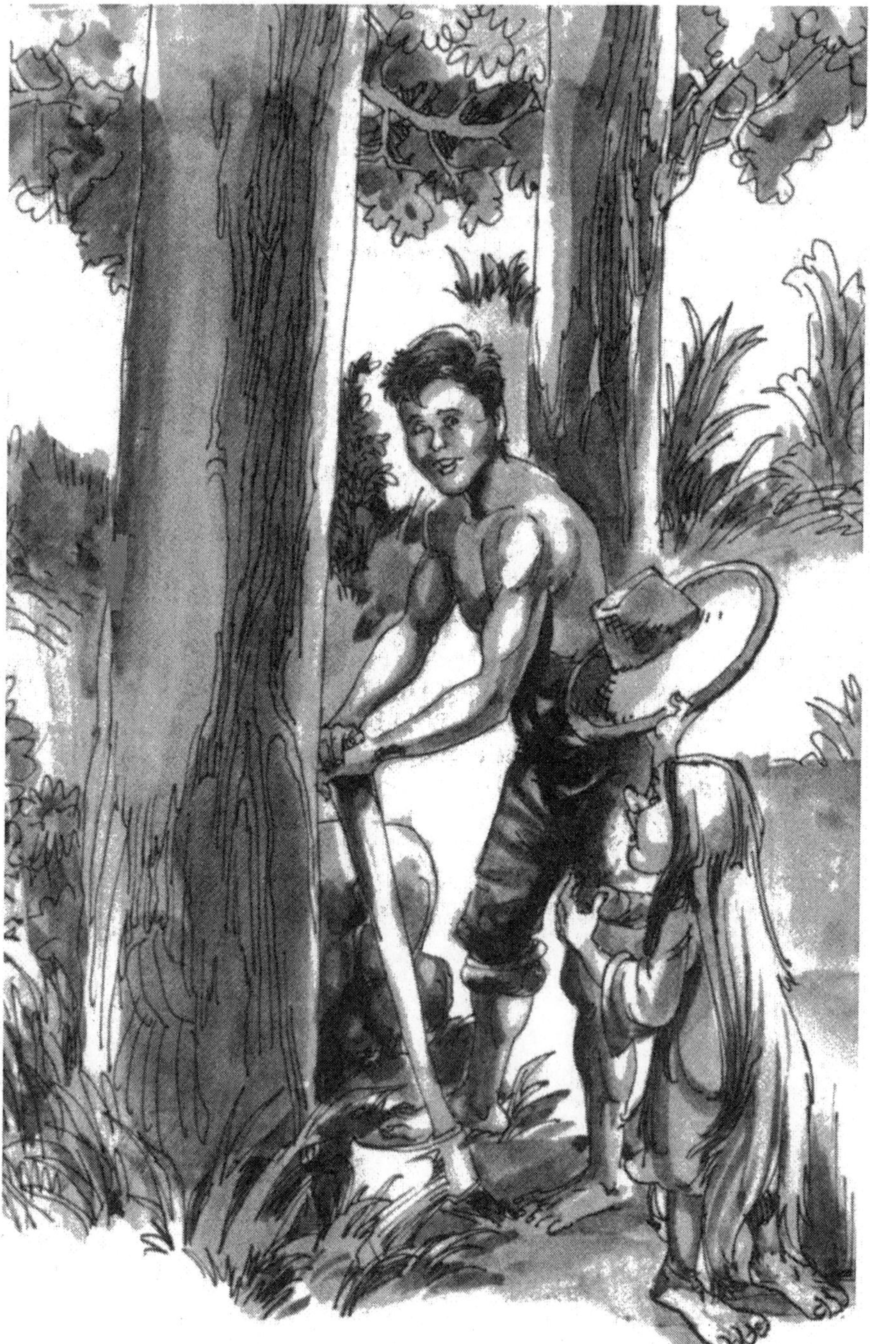

The Elf's Gifts

THERE ONCE LIVED, not far from a *bangar* tree, a fisherman and his son. The flowers of the bangar tree have a bad smell, but strange to tell, elves make their home in bangar trees although they are such dainty people.

Every year whenever the tree bloomed, the fisherman wanted to cut it down. But he was afraid that the elves living in the tree would harm him, and so he and his son patiently endured the bad smell.

One year, however, he grew so sick with the smell that he decided to cut down the tree. He sharpened his axe and proceeded to the foot of the tree. "I do not care what will happen to me for this," he told himself. "I must chop down this tree."

But when he swung his axe, a kiba-an, a pretty elf as small as a child of two years, came down from the tree. Her hair extended to her feet, and on her feet the toes were behind and the heels were before. Her skin was as white as rice, and her teeth were pure gold. She held a hat in her hand, and she turned to him and said:

"Old man, spare my tree and I will give you this hat."

"Of what good is it?" asked he.

"Nobody will be able to see you as long as you have it on."

"Then I certainly will take it," said the fisherman. He took the hat, thanked the elf, and left. On his way home he wore the hat and found that no one, not even the dogs and wild birds, could see him.

"I shall not tell my son about this hat till he is a grown-up man," thought he, hiding it. "He might do unwise things with it if he gets it before he is old enough."

The next year when the bangar tree bloomed again, the fisherman grew so sick with the smell that he set out to cut down the tree. "Perhaps the kiba-an has moved into another tree," he said.

But just as before, when he swung his axe, the elf came down. She was sitting on a chair suspended in the air, and, "Good man," said she, "spare my tree and I will give you this chair."

"Of what good is it?" he asked.

"You only have to sit on it and it will take you wherever you wish."

The man took the chair, sat on it, thanked the elf, and ordered the chair to take him home; and sure enough, the next moment he found himself right at home.

Likewise he hid the chair from his son, saying, "I shall wait till he is a grown-up man, for otherwise he might do wrong things with these unusual gifts."

Then blossomtime came again and the fisherman took his axe and set out to cut the bangar down. But just as before, when the man swung his axe, the kiba-an appeared, and this time she held a purse. "Good man," said she, "spare my tree and I will give you this purse."

"What can it do?" he asked.

"Every time you put your hand in it, it will come out full of gold."

"Give it to me," said he and, thanking her, went home with the purse. And just as before, he hid the purse from his young son.

Before many years the fisherman was bent with age and he knew it would soon be time for him to leave his son. He called for the boy and asked him to bring the hat, the chair, and the purse to his bedside. He told him about what they each could do and added: "You are a man now, Son, and I am going to leave you these three things. May you be happy!"

He was dead before the bangar tree bloomed again.

Now in the city lived the king, his queen, and their beautiful young daughter, and the fisherman's son wanted to marry the princess. He was very prosperous now because he had the magic purse. He bought an expensive carriage and six steeds and ordered costly suits for himself. Then he dressed up, put the magic purse in his pocket, and drove his carriage about the king's palace.

The king saw the young man, sent for him, and said, "Young Prince, from what kingdom do you come, and what would you like to have in our city?"

"I would prefer to tell this to your daughter the princess, King," replied the fisherman's son. "May I speak with her?"

The king thought that the young man was overbold. But he appeared very wealthy and he had no desire to drive him away. So he had him shown into the princess' chamber.

"I am a poor fisherman's son," he told her frankly. "But I have here a magic purse, and any time I put my hand in it, my hand is filled with gold. How would you like to be my wife and own this purse?"

"I shall answer your question tomorrow," she replied. "Meanwhile, leave your purse with me and I shall tell my father about it."

The young man felt satisfied, gave her the purse, and left her with a courteous bow.

But next day when he returned, the guards drove him off.

"The princess is waiting for me!" he said. "Let me in!"

"The princess ordered us to keep you out," replied the guards.

So, heavy-hearted, the fisherman's son went home. Then he remembered the hat, and he put it on and drove back to the palace. He walked past the guards unseen by anyone, and when he reached the princess' chamber, he took off the hat, bowed, and said:

"I have come back to claim my bride—thanks to this hat of invisibility. Will you be my wife now?"

"I am sorry," said she, "but I find it hard to think of marrying a fisherman's son. It is never done by princesses. However," she added with a pleasant smile, "leave your hat with me and I will think the matter over. Come back tomorrow."

The youth was so much flattered by her sweet smile that he left the hat with her and went home.

He returned next day only to be thrown out by the guards at the palace gate. He told them the princess was waiting for him, but they replied that the princess had ordered them to keep him out.

So he went home, sat on the chair, and said, "Take me right into the princess' chamber!"

In a twinkling he was at the bedside of the sleeping princess. He lifted her up gently, carried her to the chair, sat on it with her in his arms, and said, "Take us to the ninth hill from here!"

The next moment they were on a grassy slope nine hills away from the kingdom.

Soon the princess awoke, and she slapped him and scratched him and bit him when he refused to take her back to the palace.

For three days they remained on the hill quarreling. On the fourth morning, while he was asleep, she took the chair quietly and said, "Carry me back into my chamber!" and the chair did so.

Then the youth awoke and found himself alone. "This is bad!" he said. "I don't even know which is east and which is west!"

He rose and walked toward the nearest hill. He walked and walked but found neither food nor water. He was about to die of hunger and thirst when he came to a clear stream, and there on its bank stood a tree full of red fruit. Greedily he ate the fruit until his hunger was appeased.

But when he bent over the water to drink, he saw two horns standing proudly on his head. Naturally he was very much alarmed. He pulled and pulled but the horns, no matter how much he pulled them, would not come off. He fell asleep pulling them and he dreamed pulling them, but they stood as firm as ever. At last he was exhausted and his hands were wet, and the horns slipped whenever he tried to pull them off. So he picked up some of the leaves of the tree, wrapped them for holds about his horns, and pulled—and lo! the horns came off pleasantly, like tight shoes being taken off after a long walk on a sunny road.

"So this is the secret of these horns!" he said. He ate more of the fruit and then easily pulled off his new horns. "This will help me some day," thought he, and he broke off a branch bearing some fruit and carried it away with him.

A few hills farther on, when he became hungry again, he ate some of the fruit of another tree growing there. Then he saw that two fangs had grown from his jaw. However, he easily pulled them out by wrapping the leaves of the tree around them and tugging. And just as before, he broke off a branch from the tree and went on his way.

Before long he reached a hill where he found another strange tree. He wondered what its fruit would give him. So he ate some, eagerly feeling all over his body to seek unusual growths. Before long he found that he had a long tail. But he easily pulled out the tail. Then he broke off a branch from the tree and went on.

This way and that way he walked, following many roads. At last, clothed in rags and wearing long hair and a long beard, he reached his native land. The fruits had strangely remained fresh, however, and as the youth walked past the palace, the king, the queen, and the princess saw the fruits and demanded to have them.

He gave them what they wanted, for this was exactly what he wished, and then hurried away with the dry leaves. He changed from his rags, had his beard shaved and his long hair trimmed, and then waited quietly in his house by the bangar tree.

As soon as the royal family had eaten the fruits, they found that each of them had two horns, two fangs, and a long tail. "What is this!" the king exclaimed in alarm and started pulling. The queen and the princess did the same thing, and they pulled and shrieked and they shrieked and pulled, but they pulled in vain. Then they sent for the servants to help them pull and ordered the medicine men to look for remedies. But no one could help them.

Finally the king sent out a notice saying that whoever should succeed in removing the ugly growths would marry the princess. All sorts of people, young and old, in the kingdom and out of it, tried to cure them. But their horns and fangs and tails remained as firm as ever.

At last the fisherman's son took the three kinds of leaves he had brought home, walked to the palace, and easily pulled the growths out.

The princess recognized him and admitted that she had treated him shabbily. To make up for her fault, she returned his magic purse, his magic hat, and his magic chair, and then she married him. She learned to love him dearly, and they lived happily ever after.

Tales of Laughter

The Tale of Pakungo-adipen

PAKUNGO-ADIPEN was a lazy man. The only thing he loved to do was lie down in bed all day long. But for one reason or another he had all the luck, as this Ilocano tale will prove to you.

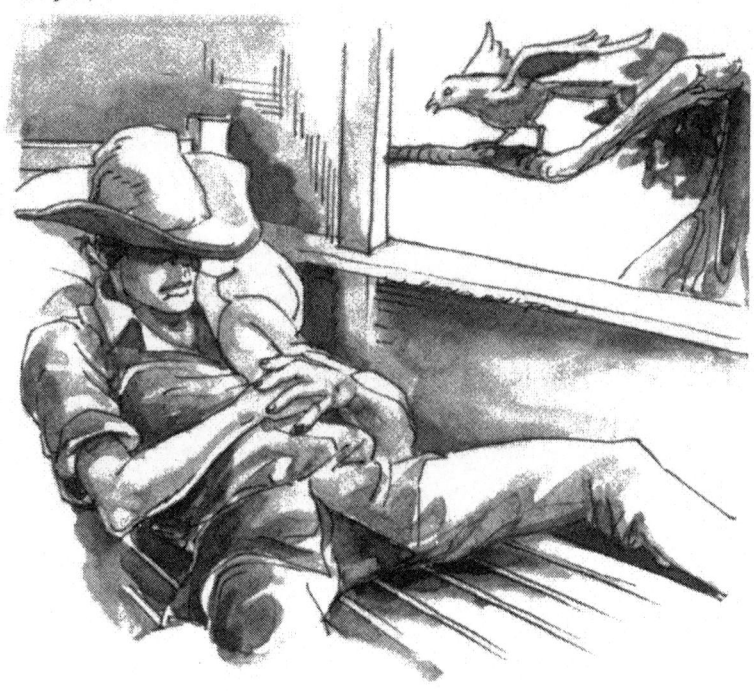

He was sound alseep one day when he heard a voice saying, "Pakungo-adipen, please shoot me down. Pakungo-adipen, please shoot me down."

He was awakened but did not mind the voice.

"Pakungo-adipen, do please shoot me down," said the voice. "Pakungo-adipen, do please shoot me down."

Reluctantly Pakungo-adipen opened one eye and saw a little bird perched on a nearby tree. "No. I am too tired to work," replied Pakungo-adipen and went back to sleep.

"Pakungo-adipen, do please shoot me down," repeated the bird. "Pakungo-adipen, do please shoot me down."

Finally Pakungo-adipen rose, much annoyed at having to get out of bed. He picked up his bow and arrow, aimed, and shot down the bird. Then he went back to bed, leaving the bird where it fell.

Hardly had he closed his eyes when the bird spoke again and said: "Pakungo-adipen, please pick me up. Pakungo-adipen, please pick me up."

He heard it but did not move.

"Pakungo-adipen, please pick me up," the bird repeated. "Pakungo-adipen, please pick me up."

"I'm too busy getting some sleep to come and pick you up," muttered Pakungo-adipen. "I won't get up just to pick up a dead bird."

"Pakungo-adipen, please pick me up," repeated the bird. "Pakungo-adipen, please pick me up."

At last Pakungo-adipen lost his temper and said, "You asked me to shoot you down, I shot you down. Now do you expect me to come and pick you up, too?"

"Pakungo-adipen, please pick me up," repeated the bird. "Pakungo-adipen, please pick me up."

At last Pakungo-adipen got up, picked up the bird, and tossed it into the kitchen. "Now I can get me a good, unbroken sleep," sighed he, lying down and falling asleep right away.

But the bird spoke again and said, "Pakungo-adipen, please dress me and cook me. Pakungo-adipen, please dress me and cook me."

Pakungo-adipen was awakened and said, "What's the matter with this bird anyway? Will it never shut its mouth?" He refused to get out of bed.

"Pakungo-adipen, please dress me and cook me," repeated the bird. "Pakungo-adipen, please dress me and cook me."

"Indeed, what kind of bird is this?" said he. "It asked me to shoot it down; I shot it down. It asked me to pick it up; I picked it up. Now it asks me to dress it and cook it, too!" But he rose with great reluctance, dressed the bird, cut it up, and left it boiling in a pot. Then he went back to sleep.

When the bird was finally cooked, it said, "Pakungo-adipen, please put me on the floor and cover me with a sheet. Pakungo-adipen, please put me on the floor and cover me with a sheet."

Pakungo-adipen heard the bird but gave it no heed.

"Pakungo-adipen, please put me on the floor and cover me with a sheet," repeated the bird. "Pakungo-adipen, please put me on the floor and cover me with a sheet."

Still Pakungo-adipen did not heed the bird.

"Pakungo-adipen, please put me on the floor and cover me with a sheet," said the bird again, and it said these words over and over until at last Pakungo-adipen sat up and said:

"What kind of bird are you, really? You wanted to be shot down, and shoot you down I did. You wanted to be picked up, and pick you up I did. You wanted to be dressed and cooked, and dress you and cook you I did. And now you expect me to put you back on the floor and cover you with a sheet? I certainly will do nothing of the sort!" he shouted and went back to sleep.

But the bird repeated, "Pakungo-adipen, please put me on the floor and cover me with a sheet. Pakungo-adipen, please put me on the floor and cover me with a sheet." It said these words over and over and over again until at last Pakungo-adipen rose, poured out the cooked bird on the floor, and covered it with a clean bedsheet. When he had done, he sighed a long sigh and said, "Now at last I can enjoy my sleep!"

But by and by he heard a sweet voice saying, "Pakungo-adipen, please uncover me. Pakungo-adipen, please uncover me."

Pakungo-adipen did not move. He closed his eyes tight and was soon snoring—for he enjoyed his sleep better when he snored.

"Pakungo-adipen, please uncover me," the sweet voice said again. "Pakungo-adipen, please uncover me. Pakungo-adipen, please uncover me."

So Pakungo-adipen got up, stamped on the floor, and said: "What bird or devil are you? You asked to be shot down; I shot you down. You asked to be picked up; I picked you up. You asked to be dressed and cooked; I dressed and cooked you. You asked to be put on the floor and covered with a sheet; I put you on the floor and covered you with a sheet. And now you expect me to come and uncover you again? No, I will do nothing of the sort! I am too busy getting me a good sleep!"

So saying, he went back to bed and was soon snoring again.

But the voice did not stop. It continued repeating: "Pakungo-adipen, please uncover me. Pakungo-adipen, please uncover me. Pakungo-adipen, please uncover me."

"Oh, I will never have peace with this bird!" moaned Pakungo-adipen, getting up at last. He staggered to where he had covered the bird on the floor, pulled off the sheet, and lo and behold!—a strange and delightful sight met his eyes. For there on the floor lay, not the bird, cooked, dressed, or shot. There on the floor lay no bird at all. There on the floor lay the most beautiful princess you ever saw or heard of. She opened her eyes, smiled, and extended her arms to Pakungo-adipen. And so surprised was Pakungo-adipen that he quite forgot to go back to sleep but took her in his arms and, to put a tail to my tale, married her.

I regret that I really do not know whether Pakungo-adipen and the princess led a happy married life. If you should press me for an answer, I should say that they probably did, for with such a sweet wife in his home, Pakungo-adipen must have learned to be ashamed to sleep too much. I have very little doubt that with such a sweet wife, Pakungo-adipen must have learned to be hard-working and wide-awake.

But then that's only my guess.

The Man and the Lizard

THIS TALE HAPPENED long, long ago, when the Mona, the first parents of mankind, according to the Bagobos of Davao, still lived on earth. At that time there lived a man and his wife, and one day the man took his snares and headed for the woods. He sought the trails of the wild chickens and there set his snares in such a way that when the wild fowls came hurrying along in search of food, they would get caught.

The following day he returned to the woods and found a lizard caught by one of his snares. "I'll make this lizard carry my things home and then be killed by my wife," thought he.

So he set the lizard free, gave him his bolo and his carrying-basket, and said: "Hurry along to my house, lizard, and take this bolo and this basket to my good wife."

"Yes, my good master," replied the lizard and scurried off.

Now the lizard knew that people liked to eat his flesh for dinner. "I do not want to fool the man," he told himself, "but neither do I want to be his dinner." So, as soon as he was safely hidden from view, he crept from the trail and climbed up a tree standing beside a stream.

The man visited his other snares but saw only loose feathers there. He did not know that the lizard had eaten up the wild chickens caught in the snares before he was himself snared.

"I have little luck today," thought the man. "But anyway I shall have the lizard for dinner." He walked home and, "Wife, let's have dinner, for I am very hungry," he said as he climbed up the ladder.

"Come right in," his wife replied. "Dinner is ready."

The man sat down to eat but saw no lizard meat. "Where's the lizard?" he asked. "Get him out of the pot and let's eat him."

"What lizard?"

"The lizard that I sent to you, of course."

"Sent to me!"

"I sent you a lizard this morning," the man explained. "Did you not cook him?"

"Whom did you ask to bring the lizard to me?"

"I asked the lizard himself. My snare caught the lizard. I asked him to bring you my bolo and my carrying-basket. But stop joking, Wife. Where are my basket and my bolo, and where is the lizard?"

"If you are joking, I am not!" she said. "If you sent the lizard to me as you say, of course he never came. He must have run away."

"Why did he do that?"

"Because no lizard who loves his life is fool enough to come and be killed for dinner. Besides, no lizard can understand human speech."

"But this lizard understood me," said the man impatiently. "He could even speak. He promised to bring home my bolo and my basket. I must go back and catch that lizard. He will pay dearly for running off just like that—and with my bolo and my basket too!"

The man walked back into the woods and soon found the lizard's tracks. He followed the tracks until he came to the stream. Looking in the water, he saw the lizard's reflection there.

"Ah, there you are!" he exclaimed. "Now I will get you!" He jumped into the water to catch the lizard. He made a big splash, and so the lizard's reflection disappeared. The man returned to the bank and watched for it to reappear. "That lizard is indeed tricky," he muttered.

By and by the water became still and the lizard's image reappeared in it. "There he is!" said the man, leaping into the water, but of course he did not catch the lizard.

When he was tired out, he went home and told his wife what happened. "I almost got him," he said. "But he is very slippery."

"I would like to see this lizard myself," said she. "Let's go and look for him."

They walked to the stream and he pointed at the lizard's image in the water. "There he is!" he said.

She looked into the water once and then up into the tree. "Why, there is your lizard, laughing at you!" she said, pointing up.

The man saw the lizard up in the tree. "Yes, indeed!" he said. "But who is the lizard in the water?"

"That is nothing but the reflection of the lizard up in the tree," she replied patiently.

"You lizard, you!" shouted the man. "Now I'll come up and get you!" So saying, he scrambled up the tree. When he got near the lizard, "Now you are going to pay with your life for disobeying me," he said. "I told you to carry home my bolo and my basket, but what did you do instead? You ran off with them!"

But when he tried to reach out for the lizard, he lost his balance, fell off the tree, broke his neck, and died.

The Man Who Played Dead

"LIFE IS VERY DULL " thought Juan one day. "Let me play a harmless trick on my neighbors and get a little laugh from it."

He covered his cart with black cloth, and in the evening when no one was around, pushed the cart to the side of a road hard by the forest. He set up candles around the cart and lighted them. Then he wrapped himself in a shroud, climbed into the cart, and lay still.

Now the people in that place believed that the dead had the power to give good luck. As Juan lay in the cart, along came a band of robbers from the forest. They saw Juan, and walked to him, and prayed:

"O dead one, grant that we shall be lucky in our venture."

Then they went to plunder a rich man in the town. They succeeded in carrying off his money bags and were very grateful to the corpse for their good fortune.

On their way back to the forest they knelt before Juan's cart again. "Grant that we shall always be as lucky as we have been tonight," said they. Then they started to divide the gold.

"I must get the largest bag of all," said one. "My work was the hardest. I had to find out who was the richest man in the town."

"It is I who must get the biggest share," replied another. "I found out where the rich man hid his gold."

"But it was I who showed you how to get the bags," said the third. "I must have the largest share."

The other robbers made similar demands, and soon they were ready to fight each other over the money. Then their captain became very angry. "This corpse is the cause of our quarrel," he said. "If it had not given us such good luck, we would not be quarreling now. We must destroy the corpse so that we may have peace." So saying, he drew his sword and aimed it at Juan's breast.

Juan of course heard him. Seeing the captain raise his sword, he jumped up in great fright.

The robbers saw him jump and thought he was a ghost. They were so scared that they fled in all directions without stopping to pick up the bags of gold.

Juan got down, put the bags of money in the cart, and pushed the cart home. From then on he lived like a man of great wealth, and he bought a big house and hired many servants.

Pedro, Juan's neighbor, saw Juan's sudden prosperity and paid him a visit. "How did you come by so much wealth, my good neighbor?" Pedro asked. "Only a few days ago you were poor, and now you are as rich as a king.

Did you find a buried treasure?"

"I found a treasure, all right," replied Juan.

"Where?"

"I'll tell you," Juan said. "I took my cart near the woods and covered it with black cloth. Then I wore a dead man's clothes, lay down in the cart, and kept still. And God took pity on me and gave me several bags of gold. Here, take some," he added, reaching into his pocket and giving Pedro several handfuls of gold.

Pedro took the gold and hurried home. Promptly he covered his cart with black cloth and put on a shroud. But he was afraid to go near the forest so late in the day. "The forest is the home of ghosts and robbers," he told himself. "Besides, I know of a better place to go."

So after dark, just as soon as there were no people in the streets, Pedro quietly pushed the cart into the church. He set up candles around the cart, climbed on, and lay still. "God will give me more money than He gave Juan," Pedro thought. "Juan only went to the woods. I came directly into God's house."

By and by the sacristan entered the church to ring the

evening bell. He saw the cart, looked into it, and was much surprised. He had not rung the bell to admit a dead man and yet here was a bier with a corpse on it! He fled from the church, ran to the convent, and told the priest what he had seen. "It's a miracle!" the sacristan said.

"You must be dreaming," said the priest.

"Come down and see for yourself, Father!" the sacristan replied.

They went inside the church, and when the priest saw Pedro lying on the cart, "Go and fetch the grave-digger," he told the sacristan, "and we shall bury the corpse."

Pedro heard him and became alarmed, for of course he did not want to be buried. So he jumped off the cart and ran away.

The priest and the sacristan saw him run away and were even more frightened than Pedro was. Out of the church they ran in opposite directions as fast as their clothes would let them.

Pedro hurried away, too. He was very thankful that he did not get buried after all. "I should have gone into the forest instead," he thought. "There God would have given me a little money, and I would not have lost my cart."

The Two Foolish Peddlers

THERE ONCE LIVED two neighbors, according to an old Ilocano tale—Oppong and Angkil. They were both too fond of the fermented juice of sugar cane called basi.

"*Pari!*" yawned Oppong to Angkil late one morning, waking up. "I have thought of an excellent way to make money."

"Tell me about it, Pari," Angkil replied, yawning from his window.

"We shall go to town and peddle basi."

"But where is the basi?" asked Angkil. "You and I have drunk all the basi in the barrio."

"We shall go to the other barrios and buy all the basi we can get."

"And where shall we get the money to buy the basi?"

"We shall sell our carabaos and return to our native village with double the money we get for them," said Oppong.

Angkil agreed and so they sold their carabaos cheap. With the money Oppong and Angkil bought all the basi found in the neighboring barrios. This they poured into a *bayeng-yeng*, or long bamboo tube, which Oppong carried across his shoulder.

They started out for town late in the afternoon just as soon as the heat of the sun had left the road. As they walked along they shouted, "Basi! Who will buy wonderful basi? Who will buy basi that drives all cares away?"

The bayeng-yeng was quite heavy and so they took turns in carrying it. Darkness had fallen over the landscape before an old woman living by the roadside stopped them and asked for a bowl of basi. She handed them a five-centavo piece in payment, and the question of who should hold the coin puzzled Oppong and Angkil. Finally they agreed that whoever happened to be carrying the bayeng-yeng when a sale was made should hold the money from that sale and hand over the bayeng-yeng to the other. Oppong took the money and put it in his pocket.

They decided to continue traveling in the dark so that they might reach town by early morning, when people drink much basi to warm their stomachs. They walked and walked until at last they grew tired and decided to rest.

"Pari," said Oppong to Angkil, who happened to be holding the bayeng-yeng at the time, "can you sell me some of the basi?"

"I don't see why not, Pari," replied Angkil. "How much will you buy?"

"Oh, just a bowl."

Angkil filled the bowl and Oppong quaffed the basi, handing the old woman's coin to Angkil and reluctantly taking the bayeng-yeng from his friend.

Then they resumed their journey. After a while Angkil said, "Pari, please sell me some of the basi, too."

"Certainly," replied Oppong. "How much?"

"No more than you drank, I suppose. Just a bowl."

Oppong filled the bowl and Angkil quaffed the wine. Then the coin changed hands and Angkil shouldered the bayeng-yeng.

They had not walked much farther when Oppong said, "Pari, some basi, please."

"A bowl of it, Pari?" asked Angkil, pleased to be relieved of the bayeng-yeng so soon.

"Yes, just a bowl," said Oppong.

Their stops for a drink of the basi became more and more frequent. At last the two friends just sat down at the roadside pouring the basi for each other. Before long they had sold and drunk all the basi between themselves. Then they staggered to a lighted hut near by. "Let's go over there and count the money we got for the basi," they said.

Animals and People

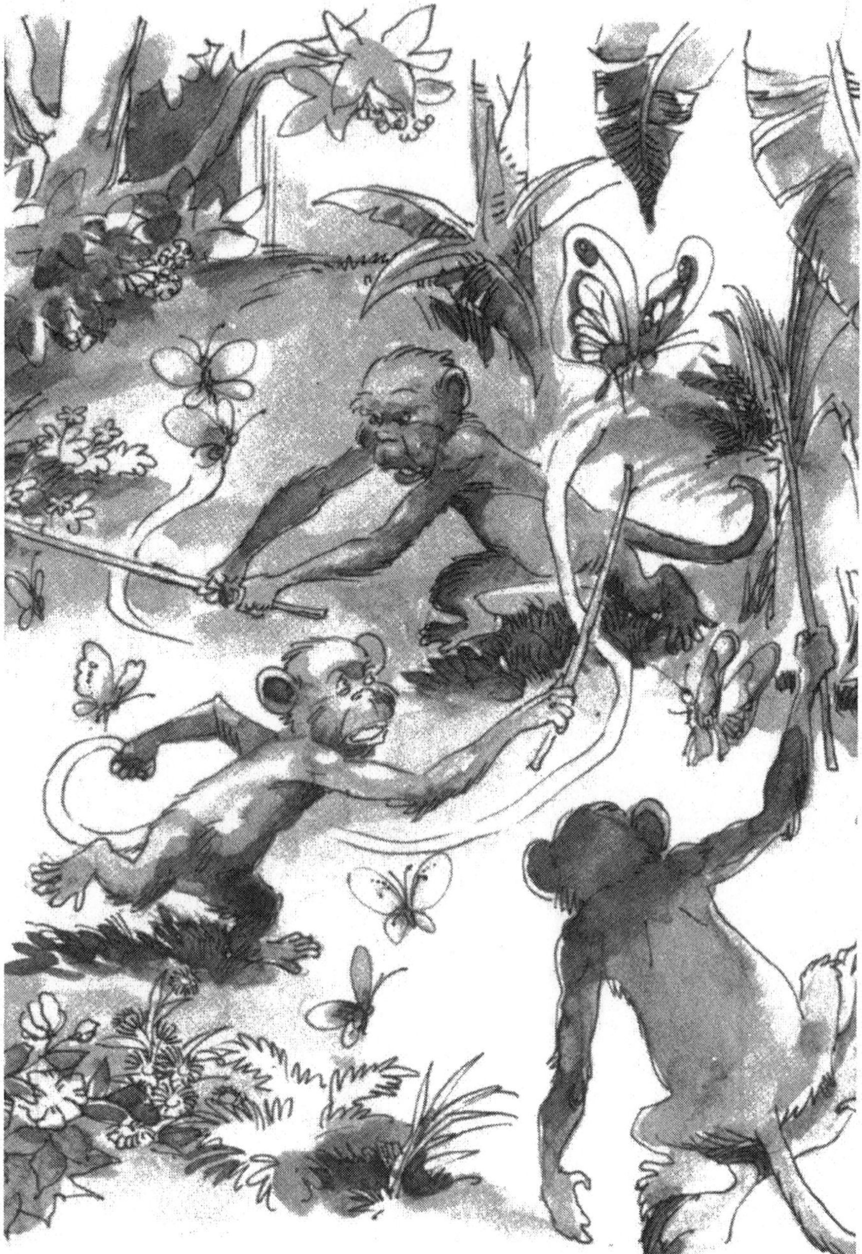

The Monkeys and the Butterflies

DEEP IN A FOREST in Agusan lived many monkeys and butterflies. They gave no trouble to each other, for while the monkeys ate the fruits of the forest trees, the butterflies drank the nectar from the flowers.

But one day the monkeys decided to kill the butterflies. "This is our forest," they said. "We want no butterflies around."

So they picked up sticks and marched to the glade where the butterflies were flitting about from flower to flower and sipping sweet nectar. There were white butterflies and black butterflies. There were red butterflies, yellow butterflies, orange butterflies, and butterflies of mixed colors. The meadow looked very gay with so many butterflies flitting among the flowers.

The monkeys rushed upon the butterflies and began hitting them with their sticks. The butterflies fell one by one, and soon only one butterfly remained.

This last butterfly flew to the top of a tree where the monkeys could not reach her. "What could my people have done to make the monkeys so angry with us?" she thought. "We have stolen nothing from them, and we have never given them any trouble. All we have done is drink nectar from the flowers. Unless we do this, the flowers will not produce seeds, and if there are no seeds, soon there will be no trees. Then the monkeys will have no fruits to eat." The butterfly grew angry and added: "I will avenge the death of my people." She flitted down and hovered just beyond the reach of the monkeys.

The monkeys saw her and said, "This is the last of the butterflies. Let us kill her and finish our job." They tried to reach her with their sticks and said, "Come nearer and we will give you a nice whack!"

To their surprise, the butterfly came closer to the ground. She flew quickly about and alighted on the forehead of the largest monkey. "Kill me if you can!" she shouted.

The monkeys raised their sticks and tried to hit her. But when they looked again, they found that the butterfly had darted off and alighted on the head of the next largest monkey. The other monkeys raised their sticks again and tried to hit the butterfly. But just as before, the butterfly darted off quickly and alighted on the head of the next largest monkey.

This went on and on, and as the butterfly flew from one monkey's head to another, the monkeys tried all the harder to hit her. They were so interested in trying to hit the butterfly that they did not see they were growing fewer and fewer. Only the butterfly saw that every monkey she alighted on was killed by the blows the other monkeys meant for her. "Kill me if you can!" she challenged them, and more monkeys were killed.

At last only one monkey remained. He was very tired trying to hit the butterfly. He stood on a rock breathing hard.

The butterfly alighted on a leaf and said to him, "Please put down your stick. I would like to have a nice talk with you."

The monkey dropped his stick and said, "What do you wish?"

"As you can see," replied the butterfly, "you are the last monkey in the forest. And I am the last butterfly, too."

The monkey nodded.

"Now, we butterflies have never done you monkeys any harm," the butterfly went on. "We are not like the mosquitoes who sting you or the fleas who bite you day and night. We only drink nectar from the flowers, and that harms nobody. On the other hand, if we do not carry pollen from one flower to another, no seeds will grow, and if there are no seeds, very soon you monkeys will have no fruit to eat. Young seeds that get no pollen do not grow."

"What do you think we should do?" asked the monkey.

"You and I should agree to let each other alone," replied the butterfly. "Just continue eating the fruits of the trees as before, but allow me and my children to sip the nectar from the flowers, too."

The monkey agreed, and since then he and the butterfly have never quarreled again.

Three Friends Seek a Home

THE PLAYERS

    Eel   Old Man
    Catfish   Wife
    Bee

SCENE I

(*The* Eel *and the* Catfish *meet on the road.*)

Catfish: A fine evening to you, Eel.

Eel: A fine evening to you, too. Why are you out so late today, if I may ask?

Catfish: I am looking for a house to live in. You yourself are out late today.

Eel: I, too, am looking for a house to live in. Would you like to come along? If we find a house we shall live in it together.

Catfish: Indeed I would like to come along with you. I want to share the same house with you in case we find one. (*The* Eel *and the* Catfish *walk down the road together. By and by they meet the* Bee.)

Bee: A fine evening to you both, Friends.

Eel and *Catfish:* A fine evening to you, too.

Bee: Where are you two going so late today, if I may ask?

Eel and *Catfish:* We are looking for a house to live in.

Would you like to come along?

Bee: Sure! I, too, am looking for a house to live in.

Eel and Catfish: Let's find a house of our own and share it together.

Bee: I would like to live in the same house with the two of you. We shall all be happy together.

(*The* Eel, *the* Catfish, *and the* Bee *walk down the road together. Soon they come to a house where an* Old Man *and his* Wife *live. The three friends whisper together.*)

Eel: This is a fine house.

Catfish: This is a fine house indeed. Let's take it.

Bee: This is the house we want. Wait for me downstairs and I shall find out who lives here.

Eel and Catfish: All right. We shall wait for you here.

(*The* Bee *flies into the house, looks around, and soon returns to his friends.*)

Bee: A man and his wife live in the house. Let us frighten them away. Then we can have the house for ourselves.

Eel: That's an excellent idea. I shall sleep on the ladder tonight. When the old man comes down early in the morning, he will step on my slippery body and fall down. He will be frightened.

Catfish: I shall sleep in the old woman's water jar.

Bee: And I shall sleep in her fire-blower.
   (*The* Eel *stays on the ladder, the* Catfish *goes into the water jar, and the* Bee *creeps into the bamboo fire-blower. Soon they all fall asleep.*)

SCENE II

Old Man: Wife, wife! It's morning. Hurry and cook breakfast while I go down and sweep the yard.
Wife: It's morning indeed, though it's still dark. Watch your step.
   (*The* Old Man *goes down and the* Wife *gets up and proceeds to the kitchen. On the ladder, the* Old Man *steps on the* Eel, *slips, and falls to the ground.*)
Old Man: Oh, someone pushed me off the ladder!
   (*The* Wife *dips water from the jar with a coconut-shell bowl. The* Catfish *wounds her with his head spikes.*)
Wife: Oh, someone pierced my hand!
   (*She blows at the fire through the bamboo tube in which the* Bee *is hidden, and the* Bee *stings her lip.*)
   Arai! The house is full of evil spirits! Husband! Where are you? (*She goes out to look for him.*)

Husband (groaning in the yard): Ouch! Ai! Ouch!
Wife: What happened to you?
Husband: Ouch! Ai! Ai! Ouch!
Wife: There are evil spirits in the house! When I dipped water from the jar, something wounded me. And when I blew into the fire, something stung me and now my lips are swollen. Tell me what happened to you.
Husband: There must indeed be evil spirits here. When I was coming down the ladder, somebody pushed me to the ground. We better leave this house.
(*In a hurry the* Old Man *and his* Wife *gather up their belongings and go away.*)

SCENE III
(*The* Eel, *the* Catfish, *and the* Bee *meet inside the house.*)

Bee: Now they are gone.
Eel: Yes, they are gone.
Catfish: So we now have a house of our own.
All Three Together: Let's live here happily together.

The Monkey Prince

THERE ONCE LIVED a great king in the Bicol provinces. His city stood beside a dark forest inhabited by witches. This king and the leader of the witches were bitter foes, and the witch-leader decided to fight his enemy by means of a wicked plan.

The king of the city had a handsome son named Ukay. Hunting in the woods one day, Ukay met a pretty maiden. He fell in love with her, not knowing that she was the witch-leader's daughter and she was herself a witch.

Ukay and the witch-maiden often secretly met in the woods, and in time he found out who she was. But so greatly did he admire her good looks that he was quite willing to forget that she was a witch. He could not marry her, however, for he was not brave enough to tell his father she was a witch.

The days went by. Ukay's father was getting old and he saw that Ukay had grown to be a young man. So he decided that Ukay should get himself a wife. "There are many fair maidens in my kingdom, Son," said he. "Why don't you choose one of them and marry her?"

Ukay looked at his father sadly and shook his head. "I am sorry I cannot marry a girl from the city," he replied.

"What's wrong with the girls from this beautiful city?" the king wanted to know. "I have watched them pass before the palace gates, and they are all very pretty."

"I am very sorry, Father," repeated Ukay, "but I just cannot marry a girl from the city."

The years rolled by and still Ukay did not marry. Nor did he tell his father that he had given his love to a witch. At length the king, who wanted to be sure that his line would continue, gathered the maidens in his kingdom together and told his son to choose his wife from among them.

But Ukay refused to choose. At last the king lost his temper and himself picked out the fairest of the maidens. "I order you to marry this maiden," said he.

Rather than make his father angry, Ukay bowed to his will and promised to wed the king's choice.

The witch-maiden heard of this and became furious. She strode to Ukay, pointed her finger at him, and said: "You are a miserable coward! You did not tell your father that you have given your love to me. Your father is a tyrant. He did not let you choose the woman you wanted to marry."

"For this," she added, her eyes flashing with hatred, "you and your people shall suffer. Your city shall become a wilderness. Your father and your people shall become beasts. And you yourself shall become a monkey. You shall live high up in a tree, and a monkey you shall be until a beautiful maiden learns to love you more than she loves herself."

So saying, she returned to the dark forest.

No sooner had she turned her back than the proud city became a wild forest. The king and all his subjects were changed into lizards, snakes, wild pigs, jungle fowl, crocodiles, and other animals of the forest. Also, just as the witch had said, Ukay became a monkey. He climbed up into a tree and said nothing but "Kra-kra-kra!" all day long.

The years dragged on one by one and Ukay and his people remained in their animal forms. The neighboring kingdoms wondered greatly why a forest had so quickly covered the famous city.

Two centuries passed, three centuries, and the great city was forgotten. People from other kingdoms came to clear the forest. Little by little the woods were cut down and houses were built where the city had once stood.

Patiently, as the decades rolled by, the monkey prince waited for a chance to win the love of a maiden so that the spell which the cruel witch had cast on him and his people would be broken. He realized that though he had lived so long, his life as an animal was not at all so interesting as his short life as a man had been.

One day the monkey prince caught a maiden in the woods and carried her off to his tree. He was very polite and gentle to her, but instead of falling in love with him, she grew ill with fright and soon died. The same thing happened to another maiden he captured soon after. The people heard about these things and avoided the forest altogether. "There is a terrible monster in this forest," they whispered to one another.

Four hundred years passed, then four hundred and fifty. One morning a beautiful maiden entered the forest with eyes filled with tears. Her lover had forsaken her and married the daughter of a rich man. So she had come into the woods to die. She sat at the foot of Ukay's tree lamenting her sad fate. "I want to die, O I want to die!" she wailed, her head bent down to her breast.

Quietly Ukay climbed down and took her tenderly by her hand. The maiden was so heart-broken that she did not mind him. She did not even notice him carry her up into the tree.

But when he spoke to her, she opened her eyes and saw him, and she jumped up in terror. She screamed and shrieked till the forest rang with her voice, but she had no way to escape. She had come to the forest to die, but now that she could have leaped to her death, she was more interested in saving her life than in ending it. She continued screaming and shrieking, but when she looked into the monkey's eyes again she found that somehow they looked like the eyes of a man of noble birth. His face, too, though hairy, resembled a man's, and she felt a little sympathy for him.

At last she stopped screaming and shrieking altogether and sat quietly on a branch of the tree.

Then the monkey offered her a ripe banana. She did not take it, but he held it out to her with so much pleading in his sad eyes that at last she accepted the banana. She took a small bite and found it good. She took another bite and then another until she had eaten the whole fruit. The monkey gave her another banana and she ate that, too.

Then she sat looking into the monkey's eyes and admiring him even more.

The days passed and her admiration changed into love. Finally her love for him was more than her love for herself.

She awoke from a long slumber on the afternoon of the tenth day to find the tree completely gone. She also found herself in a beautiful palace. The strange monkey was gone too, and a handsome young prince lay asleep near at hand. The prince soon woke up, kissed her fervently, and told her the wonderful story of his life.

At the same time the king and all his people shed off their beastly forms, and the wilderness turned into the proud city of more than four hundreds years before.

The spell cast by the witch had been broken.

Needless to say, Ukay married the maiden, and everyone was grateful for what she had done. When the king grew old and died, Ukay succeeded him, and Ukay ruled the kingdom very wisely and well indeed.

Tale of the Kind-hearted Manobo

DEEP IN THE WOODS of Bukidnon, there once lived a young Manobo. His house was built in a tall tree, and it was made of sticks, straw, and feathers. His skin was covered with sores.

He lived by trapping wild chickens and was so poor that he had to wear a coat made of chicken feathers. He would set his traps early in the morning and visit them before sundown. Since no other hunter lived in the forest, he easily managed to snare wild fowls.

One day, on visiting his traps as usual, he found them all empty. He was surprised because many of the traps had been sprung.

Again he found his traps empty next day, and he grew suspicious, for not only were the traps sprung as before but fresh feathers also lay near them.

So on the third day he concealed himself in a bush hard by his traps. He had not long to wait, for soon several wild chickens were caught in the traps. Then a large rat and a large snake came along and quietly took the chickens from the traps.

The man jumped out and ran after the thieves. He caught them as they were about to enter a hole under a tree.

"You must pay with your lives for your thieving," he said, raising his bolo.

Then the rat and the snake spoke and said, "Please

spare our lives and we will give you magic power."

"What magic power?" he asked.

The rat held out three strands of hair, and in its mouth the snake held out three clean feathers. "Take these," they said. "You only have to rub them on the dead to bring them back to life."

The man took the feathers and hair and said, "I will spare your lives if you promise never to rob my traps again."

"We promise and thank you," said the rat and the snake. "We will always remember your kindness."

Now the village chief had a beautiful daughter whom he loved so much that he did not want to marry her off early. To keep her from the eyes of admirers, he confined her in a high tower standing on a single wooden post. She was given an old woman for her attendant, and the food and clothes the two needed were sent up to them by means of a rope.

The rat and the snake learned about the imprisoned princess and determined to help her. They hurried to the foot of the tower, and quietly by night the rat started gnawing a hole up through the post. It took many nights of patient gnawing, but at last the rat reached the top of the post. Then the snake squirmed through the hole, bit the princess in the heel, and slid back to the woods with the rat, who had sat waiting for him in the grass below.

The princess fell to the floor and died, and the old woman who attended to her raised a loud cry. "Your daughter is dead, O Chief!" she wailed. "Your dear daughter is dead!"

The chief was filled with grief and he summoned his medicine men to ask for their help. They tried all the herbs and mixtures that they knew, but nothing they gave her could help the dead princess. The land was loud with mourning.

Then the chief's advisers counseled that he should make every man in his realm try to cure the princess. So the chief had a large gong beaten to summon all the men within reach of its sound. When all were gathered together, he told them about the princess's death. "Whoever can restore her to life," he said, "may marry her."

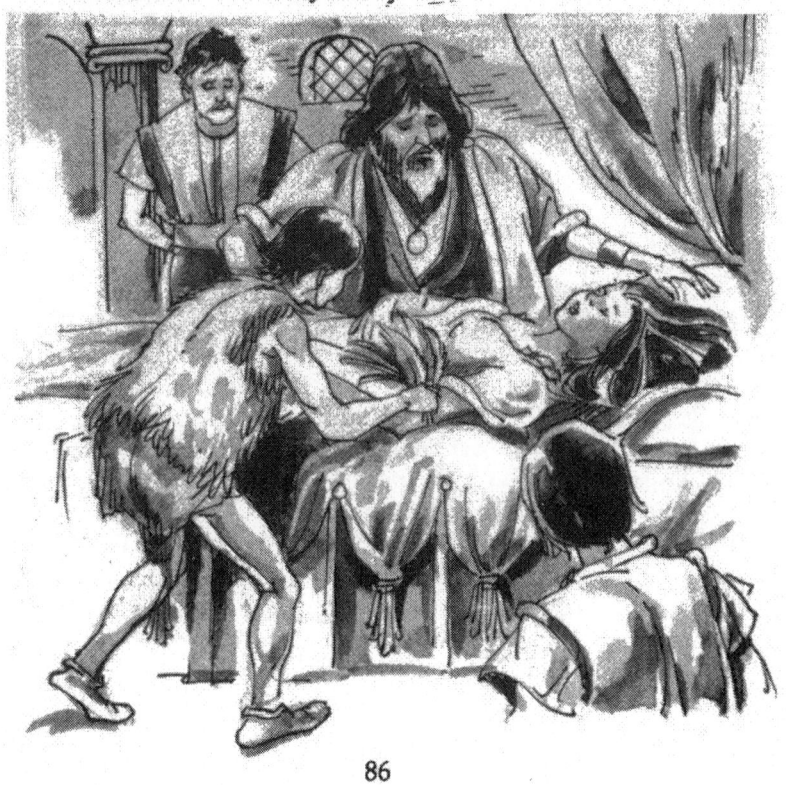

Every man tried his own cure, but none could restore the life of the princess. Then the chief asked his messengers: "Have you called in all my subjects? There must be one who can bring my daughter back from her mysterious death. Could anyone have been missed?"

"There is one we have not summoned," said the messengers. "But he is so queer that we thought he should not be called. He lives in a nest up in a tree, his clothes are made from the feathers of birds, and his skin is covered with sores. Being so sickly himself, he cannot restore the princess' life."

"Bring him in," the chief ordered them. "Perhaps he can restore my daughter to me."

So, against his will the man was brought in. He saw the dead princess and knew of nothing else to do but rub against her skin the hair and feathers the rat and the snake had given him. She stood up, opened her eyes, smiled, and began speaking as if nothing had happened.

Then the man realized that he might cure himself with the magic hair and feather, too. He touched his sores with them and immediately his skin became all clean, and he stood as handsome as a prince from a great kingdom.

Of course he married the princess, and they lived happily ever after.

The Monkey Who Became a Servant

MASOY LIVED on a small clearing beside a forest in the Eastern Visayas. He raised fruits, beans, and ginger. Every morning he would go to the village to market his products, and with the money he got he would buy rice and other things for his daily needs. In this way he lived happily, envying no one.

But early one morning when he went to his orchard to gather fruit, he saw his trees bare. "A thief must have climbed over my fence," Masoy thought, so he raised the bamboo fence.

But the fruit continued to be stolen and he grew impatient. He went to the wild wood and gathered plenty of pitch from the forest trees. He shaped the sticky pitch in the form of a man, stood it in a corner of his orchard, and put a straw hat on its head. "The thief will see the pitch-man and think it is I," thought Masoy, walking home.

By and by a monkey came along. It was this monkey who had been stealing Masoy's bananas and oranges. When he saw the pitch-man, he said to himself, "This is Masoy. I shall mock him, for anyway I can easily run away from him." Then he walked to the pitch-man and said, "Good morning, Masoy."

Of course the pitch-man did not answer.

"Won't you even return a polite greeting?" said the monkey. "Good morning, Masoy."

But still the pitch-man did not speak. So the monkey came near and slapped its face. "Take that for not returning a polite greeting!" he said. His blow fell so hard that his hand sank into the pitch-man's face. He tried to pull out his hand but it would not come off. "Won't you let go of my hand?" shouted the monkey and hit the pitch-man with his other hand.

That hand stuck, too, and, "Let go of my hands!" yelled the monkey.

But the monkey's hands would not come off, so he kicked the pitch-man, first with one foot and then with the other. This made him stick to the pitch-man completely. Then with all his might the monkey struggled to get off, but the more he tried, the more he tired himself.

By and by Masoy entered the orchard and found the monkey trapped. "Ah," said he, "so it is you who have been stealing the fruit in my orchard. Now you shall pay for your thieving."

"So this man is not you, Masoy!" said the monkey in surprise. "Now I know why he was so rude. I said good morning to him and he did not answer."

Masoy laughed. "Maybe so," he said. "But what will you say for yourself before I kill you?"

"I do not deny that I have been eating some of the fruit of your trees," replied the monkey. "But spare my life and I will serve you well."

Masoy had a naturally kind heart, and he pulled the monkey out of the pitch. From that day on the monkey became Masoy's servant. He did all the house work for Masoy and ran errands for him.

One day on his way to the village the monkey found a piece of silver and a piece of gold lying on a river bank. He went to Masoy and asked, "Master, why don't you get yourself a wife?"

"Why should I get me a wife when I can hardly support myself?" said Masoy.

"In that case, get a wife who can support you," said the monkey. "Let me try to get you a wife."

So, early next morning the monkey went to the house of the village chief and said, "Honored chief, please lend me a rice measure."

"What will you do with a rice measure, my good friend?" asked the chief.

"My master has some money he has no time to count," replied the monkey. "He thinks he better measure it instead."

"Very well," said the chief and loaned him a well-polished coconut shell used for measuring rice.

The monkey told Masoy nothing about it, but next day, before returning the measure to the chief, he carefully stuck the silver piece to the bottom of the measure. He held the measure before the chief so that he would see the piece of silver.

"There is a silver piece at the bottom of the measure," said the chief. "Take it back to your master."

"If my master was so careless as to leave it in your measure," said the monkey, "keep it for yourself."

"No, take it back to your master," the chief insisted.

"Forget it," said the monkey. "A man who has to measure his money because he cannot count it would not care about a single piece of silver."

After the monkey left, the chief wondered who his master was. He had never heard of anyone so rich that he measured his money instead of counting it.

The monkey returned a few days later and asked if he could borrow the measure again.

"What will your master do with the measure this time?" the chief asked.

"He cannot count his money and has to measure it instead," said the monkey.

The chief did not know whether the monkey's master would measure his silver a second time. But next day when the monkey returned the measure, he was astounded to see a piece of gold sticking to its bottom. "Your master left this gold," he said. "Take it back to him."

The monkey shook his head and said, "A man who has to measure his gold instead of counting it would not care about a single piece."

Now the chief became really excited. "Who is your master," he asked, "and how much money has he?"

"He owns some money, but I am sorry I cannot tell you about it," replied the monkey. "Why don't you make him your son-in-law? Then you will get to know how rich he is."

The chief thought the matter over and said, "That is a good idea. But first I must see your master. Send him to me."

"I will do that," said the monkey and left. As he crossed the river he saw a rich merchant bathing. He found the merchant's clothes on the river bank, stole them, and ran home with them. "The merchant has many clothes and does not need them all," thought the monkey. "He will not become poor by losing just these clothes, but my master may become rich by wearing them."

"Where did you get such splendid clothes?" Masoy asked when the monkey got home with them.

"I am your servant and must serve you the best way I can," replied the monkey. "Do not ask any questions, but do what I ask you to do. Change into these clothes and follow me."

So Masoy bathed, put on the merchant's clothes, and walked to the village with the monkey. They took a new path so the merchant would not see them.

The chief saw Masoy and he was well pleased with him and asked, "Have you a palace?"

The monkey made a sign to Masoy, and Masoy replied, "Yes, your Honor."

"I should like to come and pay you a visit," said the chief.

"It would be a great honor to me, sir," replied Masoy, still following the monkey's signals.

"Would it be all right if I came this afternoon?"

"Yes, sir. You would be very welcome, sir," said Masoy.

Then the monkey hurried out, leaving Masoy behind. He told the people whom he passed beside the road that if anyone should ask whose lands they tilled and whose cattle they used for work, they should say that everything belonged to Masoy. "Otherwise, the chief will get angry, and an angry chief is a cruel man," the monkey warned them.

The people promised to do so, and the monkey hurried along until he came to a large palace hidden in the woods. Now the monkey had often seen this palace before he became Masoy's servant, and he knew it belonged to a powerful evil witch. No one ever entered the palace and came out alive. The monkey stopped at the palace gate and immediately started digging a pit there.

By and by the witch came out. She saw the monkey and demanded, "Why do you dig a pit at my gate?"

The monkey ignored her and continued digging.

"I say, why do you dig a pit at my gate?" the witch repeated.

The monkey dug on without a word.

"Hey!" shouted the witch. "Tell me why you dig near my gate. Speak or you will be sorry!"

Then the monkey looked up and said, "The great chief is coming this way with his whole army. So I must dig me a hole to hide in. Be off with you now, for I have work to do in a hurry." Then he resumed his digging.

The witch became alarmed and said, "My friend, be good and let me share the pit with you."

"I do not want anyone to share this pit with me," the monkey replied. "Time is running short and I cannot dig a pit big enough for two. Dig yourself another pit."

"I will do nothing of the kind!" shouted the witch. "I will take this pit from you."

So saying, the witch jumped into the pit and pushed the monkey out. Then the monkey quickly pushed large rocks into the pit and the witch was killed.

Meanwhile, the village chief was walking thither with Masoy. As he passed along the road, he asked the people whose lands they tilled and whose cattle they worked with.

"They are Masoy's, honored Chief," said they all. They saw him smile happily to hear their words, and they felt happy, too.

Soon the chief and Masoy met the monkey. He led them into the witch's palace. The chief believed everything the monkey said. He was delighted to find that his future son-in-law had so much wealth, for the monkey showed him all the gold hidden in a pit under the witch's palace. So, to tell a long tale fast, Masoy married the chief's daughter.

I do not know whether the chief ever found out the trick the monkey played on him, but I am pretty sure Masoy and his wife lived happily with their faithful servant the rest of their lives.

Adventure Tales

Death and Datu Omar

THERE ONCE LIVED, upon a time, a poor man named Omar. He was a rich man's servant, but no matter how hard he worked and how honestly he served, he remained poor.

At last he felt discouraged and decided that to die would be better than to go on living. Since the laws of his people, the Maranaos, did not allow a man to kill himself, he walked to the house of the village chief, stood before the men gathered there, and said:

"I want to die rather than go on living. Let one of you draw his kris and slay me."

The chief and his men heard him and replied, "The laws of our land forbid a man to kill his neighbor. If you want to die, the river is brown with crocodiles, and they are hungry."

Omar walked to the river and found scores of crocodiles sunning themselves in the water and waiting for prey to come along. He went to the place where they lay thickest, leaped into the water with a big splash, and waited to be devoured.

But the beasts kept still, and not one of them moved to eat him. Omar waited impatiently and then swam to the largest of the crocodiles. But they all fled when he came near, and they hid in their caves, leaving him alone in the water.

Omar returned to the village and told the men what happened. "Show me how I might kill myself," he pleaded.

"A furious typhoon is coming," said the men. "It will uproot many trees. Go to the forest and you will be crushed to death."

Omar hurried to the woods and stood under a dead tree which he knew would fall at the first gust of wind. Soon the typhoon descended and knocked down all the trees about him. But his tree remained standing. He saw a big tree about to crash to the ground, and he ran and stood under it. As soon as he got there the tree he had just left fell with a loud crash, but the tree over his head stopped in its fall and remained leaning halfway to the ground. Soon the typhoon blew over, and in desperation Omar ran about, knocking his head against the fallen trees, trying to kill himself. At last, cold and exhausted but still alive, he fell to the ground and fainted.

Then to him there appeared a stranger in yellow robes who said, "What made you lie down here, Omar? It is wet and cold."

"I have come here seeking death," replied Omar. "For to me death would be much sweeter than life."

"It's not your time to die," said the stranger. "You are young and strong. Rise, pick up your tools, and be a tiller of the soil. When it is your time, death will come for you. Rise, and live on."

So saying, the stranger walked off and then Omar awoke. To his surprise, when he opened his eyes he found at his side a plow and other farm tools, none of which had been there before. He picked them up, walked back to the village, and became a farmer.

It did not take long before he grew wealthy. He became the datu of the village, owned much land, and had a large and happy family. No one in that community had more influence than Datu Omar, and none had more honor than he.

One night, years later, while Datu Omar lay asleep in his room, there appeared an old man who beckoned to him and said:

"Omar, your hour has come."

"My hour?" said Datu Omar. "I do not know of what you speak."

"Your hour has come," repeated the stranger. "Rise and come with me."

Datu Omar jumped out of bed, pointed to the door, and shouted, "Leave this house! I do not know you!"

"Omar, arise and come with me," repeated the stranger firmly. "The hour of your death has come."

"Leave!" yelled Datu Omar. "Life is very dear, and I do not want to come with you."

Then the stranger, who was Malakalmaut (or Death) himself, gave him such a masterful stare that Datu Omar sank to his knees and begged:

"Give me time to get ready to die. Please let me live just a month longer."

The stranger granted his request and left. "I shall come for you when the month is over," said he.

The following morning Datu Omar gathered his tenants together and ordered them to erect a high tower. The men labored in much hurry, and before the month was out, the tower stood high up above the coconut trees. "Let Malakalmaut come," he said. "He cannot climb up so high."

But when the month ended, while Datu Omar lay asleep in his room at the top of the tower, he was awakened by a voice in the middle of the night. He opened his eyes and saw Malakalmaut standing over him. "Your month is up," said Death.

But still Datu Omar did not want to go with Malakalmaut. First by means of threats and then by pleading, he tried to send Death away, but Death did not heed him. Finally Datu Omar begged, "Give me another week. I am not yet ready to leave this pleasant world of men."

Death granted him his second request, and Datu Omar spent the week putting up bars in the windows of his tower. When the week was about to end, he double-barred the doors, fastened the windows, posted heavy guards at the gate, and said:

"Death cannot enter now."

But promptly at midnight, when the week was over, Death appeared in his room and said, "Your time is up, Omar. Come with me."

In terror Datu Omar jumped out of bed, bolted out of the room, and fled from the tower. "Death is an old man," he said hopefully as he ran out of the village. "He cannot follow me. I know a cave where he will never find me."

He ran into the forest, taking devious ways, concealing himself behind rocks and trees. But when he entered the cave, there stood Malakalmaut waiting for him.

So Datu Omar fled again, but every time he stopped and felt that he had finally shaken off Death, there Death stood, sternly facing him. He ran to this place and to that, like a man who had lost his mind, until he met a woman wearing white mourning clothes.

"Whom do you mourn, my friend?" asked Datu Omar, for he recognized her as his neighbor.

"I mourn the chief of my village," she replied. "Datu Omar was such a good neighbor!"

Hearing this, Datu Omar became more alarmed than ever and ran on. Soon he met a woman carrying a jar of water. "I am very tired and thirsty," said he, begging her for a drink.

"You may have a little of this water," she said. "I need it to wash a dead man's body."

"Tell me who is dead," he said, for he recognized her, too, as a woman of his village.

"You have not heard of Datu Omar's death?" asked she. "Datu Omar was a good man."

This frightened Datu Omar still more, and he ran again, trying to flee from Death. Before long he came to some men digging in the ground. "Why do you men dig in such a hurry?" he asked them.

"Indeed, why do we dig his grave?" the men asked themselves. "Why do we bury our chief, who was such a good man?" Then the men started to weep.

At this Datu Omar ran again, and soon he came upon some carpenters making a long wooden box. "Poor Datu," they mourned, "he was such a good man. But all—the fairest along with the homeliest—die." And they, too, wept.

Then Datu Omar knew that Death was beyond his escaping. His strength left him completely, and down he sank to his feet and lay on the ground.

Death had taken Datu Omar.

The Man Who Reached the Sky-World

THERE ONCE LIVED in Ifugao a prosperous man named Bang-gilit. He had four rice granaries but he was not content to stay at home looking after his property. He loved nothing so much as a good hunt, so one day before sunrise he took two of his best hunting dogs and headed for the forest to hunt.

From early morning till the leaves of the forest were wet with dew he hunted, but he did not have much luck that day. Night fell before he knew it and he found that he had lost his way deep in the woods. So he called for his dogs.

The dogs did not come, however, and since there was no one to guide him home, he sat down under a tree, built a fire, cooked supper, and ate.

One of the dogs arrived after a while and sat by the fire. "Wait till I finish supper and then you will lead me home," said Bang-gilit to the dog as if it could understand human speech.

After he finished his supper he held his dog in leash and let it trot ahead of him.

By and by the dog perked up its ears and yapped several times. His other dog answered with another yapping from the distance, and the first dog led Bang-gilit to where the second had barked, but they did not find the other dog.

They walked on and on until they reached the edge of the forest and came to a strange, brightly lighted town. There Bang-gilit's second dog sat waiting for them. "I wonder what town this is?" thought Bang-gilit. "I do not remember ever having been here before, and I have been to many places."

Many people were about, walking or talking among themselves, and Bang-gilit stood looking on with his dogs. The streets were wide and brightly lighted and the houses were large and airy.

Some people gathered around Bang-gilit and said to one another: "Perhaps this man has just arrived in our town. We have never seen him before." Then they turned to him and said: "Where were you hit? Who speared you?"

"I was not speared at all," said Bang-gilit, shaking his head. "I am a peaceful man and have never been in battle."

"How did you meet your death then?" they asked.

"I did not die," replied Bang-gilit. "I am a peaceful citizen from the land of the Ifugaos, and my name is Bang-gilit."

"Then why are you in this town?" they asked. "Only the dead come here."

"I was hunting in the woods and night fell before I could find my way home," he explained. "My dogs were missing and I cooked supper and ate. One of my dogs returned while I was eating. I fed it and then took it in leash and we followed a footpath. By and by my other dog barked in the distance. We went after it but did not find it till we arrived here. The dog sat waiting for us at the edge of your town."

"But, man, only the souls of the dead reach this town," said they. "This is the Sky-World. We are the souls of the dead."

Bang-gilit was amazed to hear this. But the people here looked so much like those in the Earth-World that he saw no reason to get frightened. "What do you suggest I should do?" he asked them. "I am not dead, and therefore I ought not to be here."

"Come with us," said the people. "Let us show you where we of the Sky-World live."

So along the wide streets of the town they led Bang-gilit and his dogs and he saw many more airy houses where the people of the Sky-World lived.

"Do you like the Sky-World?" they asked him after a while.

"I must say you have a very beautiful town," he replied. "But I am sorry I can stay only a short time here. I should like to return to my people after four days."

"Do you mean four Sky-World days or four Earth-World days?" they asked.

Bang-gilit was puzzled at this question and asked what they meant. "Are there two kinds of days?" he asked.

"You see," they explained, "a day in the Sky-World is as long as a year in the Earth-World. Four Sky-World days would be quite a long time to people in the Earth-World."

"It is hard to believe what you say," said Bang-gilit, shaking his head and smiling in disbelief. "But however it may be, I will stay here only four days."

"You will find out what we mean when you go back to your people," said they.

Bang-gilit remained four days in the Sky-World. He visited other towns there and found them all quiet and clean and peaceful. He worked in the rice field, too—for you must know that even spirits raise rice for their food. In payment for his work he was given four porcelain jars.

Then the people of the Sky-World spoke to him and said: "You have been here exactly four days. Do you still want to go home, or would you rather remain in the Sky-World with us?"

"I have found the Sky-World a very pleasant place to live in indeed," said Bang-gilit. "But my wife and children are waiting for me down in the Earth-World. They must be very anxious to see me, especially if, as you say, four days up here is four years in the Earth-World. Please let me return to my own people."

"Just as you wish," said they.

Then they pointed to a ladder and told him to climb

down. "Walk on after you reach the foot of the ladder," they said, "and by and by you will reach your native village."

Bang-gilit thanked them for having been so kind to him. He called his dogs and took the jars.

It happened that he slipped on the way to the ladder and dropped his four beautiful jars. The jars broke to pieces and he had to leave them behind.

Soon he reached the foot of the ladder and found that it rested right on top of a tall areca-nut tree. With his dogs he slid down the tree, reached the ground, and heard the cocks crowing and saw the village folk just waking up from sleep. The smoke from early cooking rose slowly from some of the grass roofs. He was back in his native village.

His wife wept for joy when she saw him. She awakened her children, saying: "Your father is home! Your dear father is home!"

The children had all grown bigger and did not recognize him. The other village folk heard about his return and came to bid him welcome. "Welcome home, Bang-gilit!" they said. "Welcome home to the village!"

Then Bang-gilit told them his strange story. Not everybody in the village believed it, but all agreed that it was a most interesting tale. "We are indeed happy to see you back home!" they said. "Where have you really been?"

The Buried Treasure

ONCE THERE LIVED a poor farmer and his wife. Their farm was so small and the soil so poor that the beans, tomatoes, and eggplants they raised were barely enough for their daily needs.

To make it worse for them, one day the husband became ill. So the wife had to do the work all by herself. She would leave the house early after breakfast and be out working in the field all day.

She was weeding the plants one morning when she found a copper coin in the grass. She weeded some more and found another copper coin. Then she found still another. This went on until she had a hundred copper coins in all.

On her way home in the evening, she bought some rice with the money. She did not tell her husband about what she found. "He might think I stole the money," she thought. "If I keep quiet about it there will be no trouble."

In the field next day she found a silver piece among the weeds. She weeded some more, and upon reaching the edge of the field where bamboos and large trees grew, she heard a voice say:

"Do not breathe a word to anyone about your good fortune and you will find more treasure."

The woman walked home, buried the silver piece in a hole, and put a stone over it so that she would remember where it was. She found another piece in the field next day and another the next, and this went on until she had a handful of silver pieces. She hid them all with the first one.

She returned to the field on the seventh day and found nothing more. At noon she walked to the edge of the field where large trees grew. There she gathered three stones, made a stove with them, and built a fire. Over the fire she placed a pot of rice to cook. Before the rice started to boil, she heard the voice again, and it said:

"Never mind boiling the rice. Dig right under the fire and you will find all the gold you need. But be sure to say not a single word about it to anyone."

The woman took the pot from the stove, scattered the burning faggots, and began digging in the ground where the fire had been. It did not take long before she struck something hard, and digging carefully some more, she uncovered a very old clay jar as large around as she could encircle with her arms.

She was full of excitement. She took off the lid from the jar and saw that it was filled with shining pieces of gold. "What good fortune I have!" she whispered to herself. She reached down to the bottom of the jar and found that it contained nothing but gold.

She did not know what to do with so much wealth. She took only two pieces, covered the jar with earth and dry leaves, and hurried home.

She was a faithful wife, and the longer she kept the secret from her husband, the more it troubled her. She would lie awake in bed at night thinking how she might continue to keep the secret from him without feeling that she had been unfaithful.

At last, after he got well again, she could keep the secret no longer. She spoke to him one night and said, "Husband, I have been hiding something from you."

He looked at her sharply and said, "Have you been unfaithful?"

"I have been faithful to you, as God knows," she replied. "But there is a secret I have hidden from you because I was made to promise that I would tell nobody about it."

"If you are faithful to me as you say, tell me your secret," he said.

So she told everything to him—not only about the coins she found in the grass while weeding the plants but about the buried treasure as well.

"We shall keep the secret all to ourselves, and no harm done," said the husband after he heard her wonderful story.

In the dead of night, when no one was stirring, they hurried to the edge of the field to dig up the jar of gold. But to their dismay, the jar had vanished. Likewise the gold she had taken home and the coins she had hidden were gone.

So the farmer and his wife became as poor as they had always been. They felt bitter, too, for they knew they could have been very prosperous if the wife had only known how to keep a harmless secret.

The Tale of Magbaloto

THERE ONCE LIVED, deep in the mountains, a man named Magbaloto. Going to the brook one morning, he came upon three beautiful women bathing. He saw their wings on the grassy bank and then he knew that they were elves. He crept to the bank when they were not looking and stole the pair of wings belonging to Makaya, the youngest elf.

Soon they finished bathing and looked for their wings. Makaya could not find her wings and began to weep. Her sisters helped her look for them but they were nowhere to be found. "We have to leave you," said they, putting on their wings. Then they flew home to the sky, and poor Makaya sat on the bank weeping bitterly.

Now Magbaloto, having hidden the wings safely, walked to Makaya and said, "Why do you weep, fair maiden?"

"Ask me no questions if you will not help me," she replied.

"How shall I help you unless you tell me what your trouble is?" he asked.

Makaya told him that she and her sisters had come to bathe in the stream and she had lost her wings. "My sisters have flown home," she sobbed, "and I cannot fly."

Then Magbaloto lied to her and said, "I am sorry but I know nothing about your wings. I am just a mortal, and what you cannot find, much less can I. But I have my home not far from here," he added, "and if you come and live with me, I shall be most happy to take you."

Makaya thought it over, and knowing that she could do nothing else, she said, "Thank you. I shall be glad to go with you."

So the elf and the mortal were married. Before another year came, they had a baby, and it was fair like its immortal mother, so that Magbaloto was very happy.

One day, while Magbaloto was harvesting rice and Makaya was rocking her baby to sleep, she saw a bundle half hidden in the thatched roof. She reached up for the bundle and opened it, and she found her missing wings there. Hastily she put them on and, leaving the baby, she flew away to rejoin her people.

Magbaloto returned and found Makaya gone. She did not reply when he called her and he found that her wings were gone, too. "Alas, Makaya has left me and our baby!" he lamented bitterly. He determined to find her, and leaving the baby with a cousin, he set out to look for his wife.

He walked and walked until at last he met the North Wind. "Why do you weep, Son?" asked the North Wind.

"Ask not why I weep unless you promise to help me," said Magbaloto.

"I cannot help you unless you tell me what gives you

trouble," replied the North Wind.

Magbaloto told the North Wind what had happened and added, "Tell me the way to heaven so that I might seek Makaya."

The North Wind shook his head and said, "Son, I have traveled far and wide but I do not know the road to heaven." But he pointed to the east and added, "Walk this way until you meet my brother the East Wind. He may be able to help you. Good luck!"

Magbaloto walked weeping toward the east until he met the East Wind.

"Why do you weep, Son?" asked the East Wind.

"Ask not why I weep unless you promise to help me," replied Magbaloto.

"I cannot promise unless you tell me what is giving you trouble."

So Magbaloto told his story to the East Wind. "Tell me the way to heaven," he added, "so that I may go and find Makaya there."

But the East Wind shook his head sadly and said, "Son, I have traveled far and near but I do not know the way to heaven." Then he pointed to the south and added: "Walk this way until you meet my brother the South Wind. Maybe he will be able to help you. Good luck!"

Magbaloto walked to the south as the East Wind had told him, and he walked and wept, and walked and wept some more until he met the South Wind, who stopped him and said:

"Why do you weep, Son?"

"Ask not why I weep," replied Magbaloto, "unless you pledge to help me."

"I know not how to help you if you do not tell me what gives you trouble," said the South Wind.

So Magbaloto told him his story, but just like his brothers, the South Wind did not know the way to heaven. "Walk this way," he added, pointing to the west, "until you meet my brother, the West Wind. Perhaps he can help you."

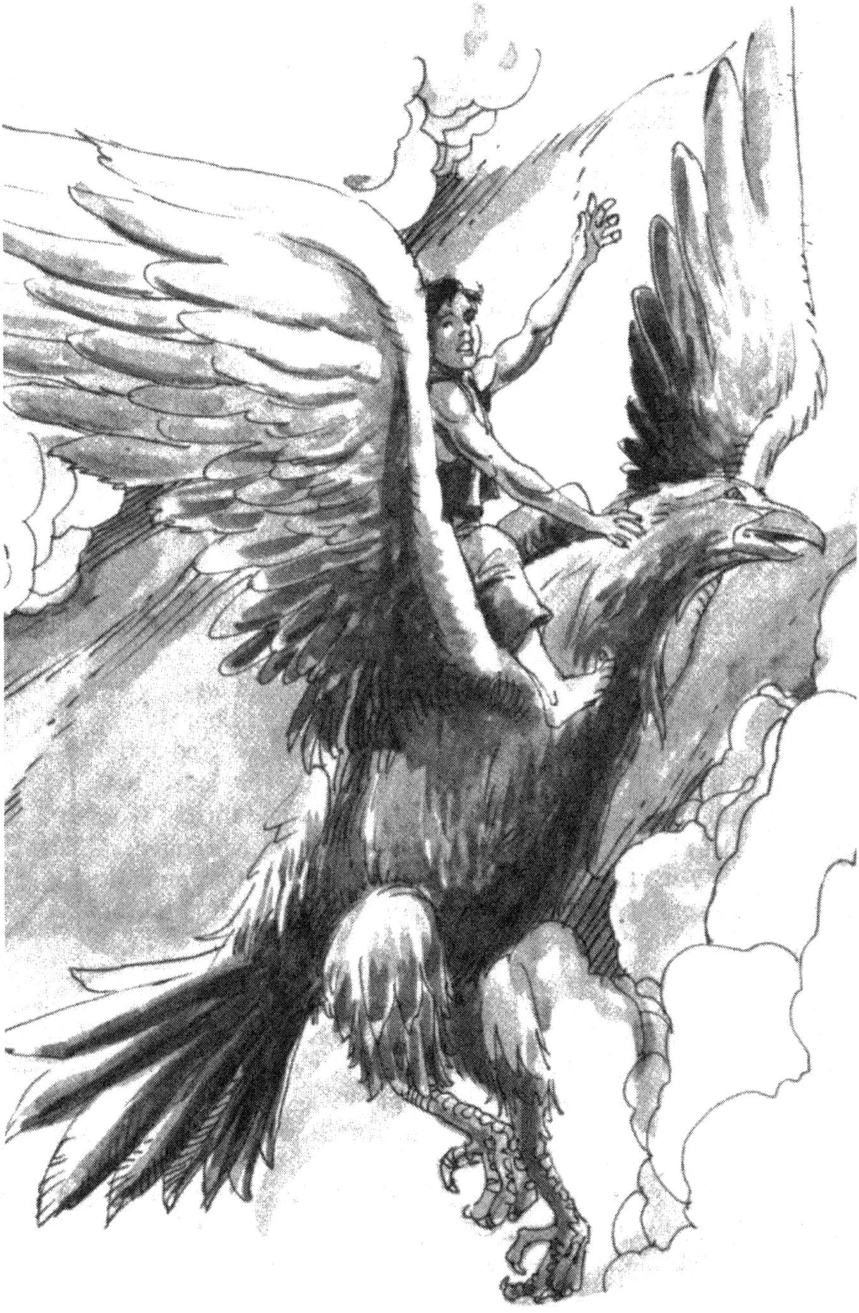

Magbaloto walked and wept some more, and at last he met the West Wind. Magbaloto told him his trouble and the West Wind said, "I do not know the way to heaven, but my friend the Eagle might. Walk on until you meet him."

So Magbaloto walked and wept some more until at last he met the Eagle.

"Why do you weep, Magbaloto?" the Eagle asked.

"Do not ask me why I weep unless you promise to help me," said Magbaloto.

"I do not see how I can promise if you do not tell me your trouble," said the Eagle.

Magbaloto told his story again, and when he had finished, the Eagle said:

"Get on my back and I will take you straight to heaven."

Magbaloto climbed on the Eagle's back and the Eagle spread his great wings and flew. They flew up, and up, and up until they reached the sky. There the Eagle rested on the top of a high mountain and said, "Get off now and seek her whom you love. I shall wait for you here."

Down the streets of the sky Magbaloto walked and walked until he came to Makaya's house. He found her with her grandmother, but when he begged the old woman to let him take Makaya to Earth with him, she replied:

"You shall not take my granddaughter from me unless you spread ten jars of sesame on the sand to dry and then gather them up again before nightfall."

With a heavy heart Magbaloto spread the sesame on the sand, and in the afternoon, as soon as they were dry, he started gathering them as fast as he could. He had gathered no more than a few handfuls, however, when the sun began to set. So he sat down and wept.

Along came the King of the Ants and asked, "Why do you weep, Son?"

"Ask not why I weep," replied Magbaloto, "unless you pledge to help me."

"How shall I help you unless you first tell me your trouble?" said the King of the Ants.

So, from beginning to end, Magbaloto told his story again. "Now the sun is about to set," he added, "and the seeds are not gathered. What shall I do!"

"Stop weeping," said the King of the Ants. He blew his horn and instantly, from north to south and from east to west, millions of ants, all the King of the Ants' subjects, came running. Their king told them what to do, and before the sun had fully set, all the sesame seeds had been gathered into the ten jars. Magbaloto took the jars to Makaya's grandmother.

But next morning, when he returned to claim Makaya, the old woman frowned at him again and said: "You shall not have my granddaughter unless you hull a hundred big sacks of rice. And you must hull the rice in a single day," she added.

Magbaloto heard this and did not know what to do, for of course he could not hope to hull more than a sack of rice in one day. So he sat down to weep.

Along came the King of the Rats and said, "Why do you weep, Son?"

"Ask not why I weep," said Magbaloto, "if you do not promise to help me."

"How can I help you if you do not tell me your trouble?" said the King of the Rats.

Magbaloto related his misfortune from start to finish again, and the King of the Rats summoned his subjects. They came scurrying at once, from south to north and from west to east, and their King ordered them to gnaw off the hulls from the rice grains. Before sunset the work was done, and Magbaloto thanked the rats and took the hulled rice to Makaya's grandmother.

But just as before, when he returned to claim his wife in the morning, the old woman scowled and said, "You shall not have my granddaughter unless you first cut down all the trees on the mountain that you see from my window. And you must finish cutting them down before sunset."

There were thousands of trees on the mountain, and after he had cut down a few trees, Magbaloto knew there was no use trying to finish the task. So he sat down and wept over his hard luck.

Along came the King of the Wild Pigs and said: "Why do you weep, Son?"

"Ask not why I weep," replied Magbaloto, "unless you promise to help me."

"How can I promise to help you if you do not tell me your trouble?" asked the King of the Wild Pigs.

Magbaloto told his story again, from first to last. Then the King of the Wild Pigs called his subjects. From east to west and from north to south they all came and cut down all the trees with their sharp tusks.

When, next morning, Magbaloto went to claim Makaya a third time, her grandmother got tired of trying to think of more difficult tasks for him to do. So she said, "Take her with you if you wish." Makaya followed him gladly, for she, too, longed to return to her baby.

The Eagle met them at the mountain. They climbed on his back and flew down to Earth, and there they lived happily ever after.

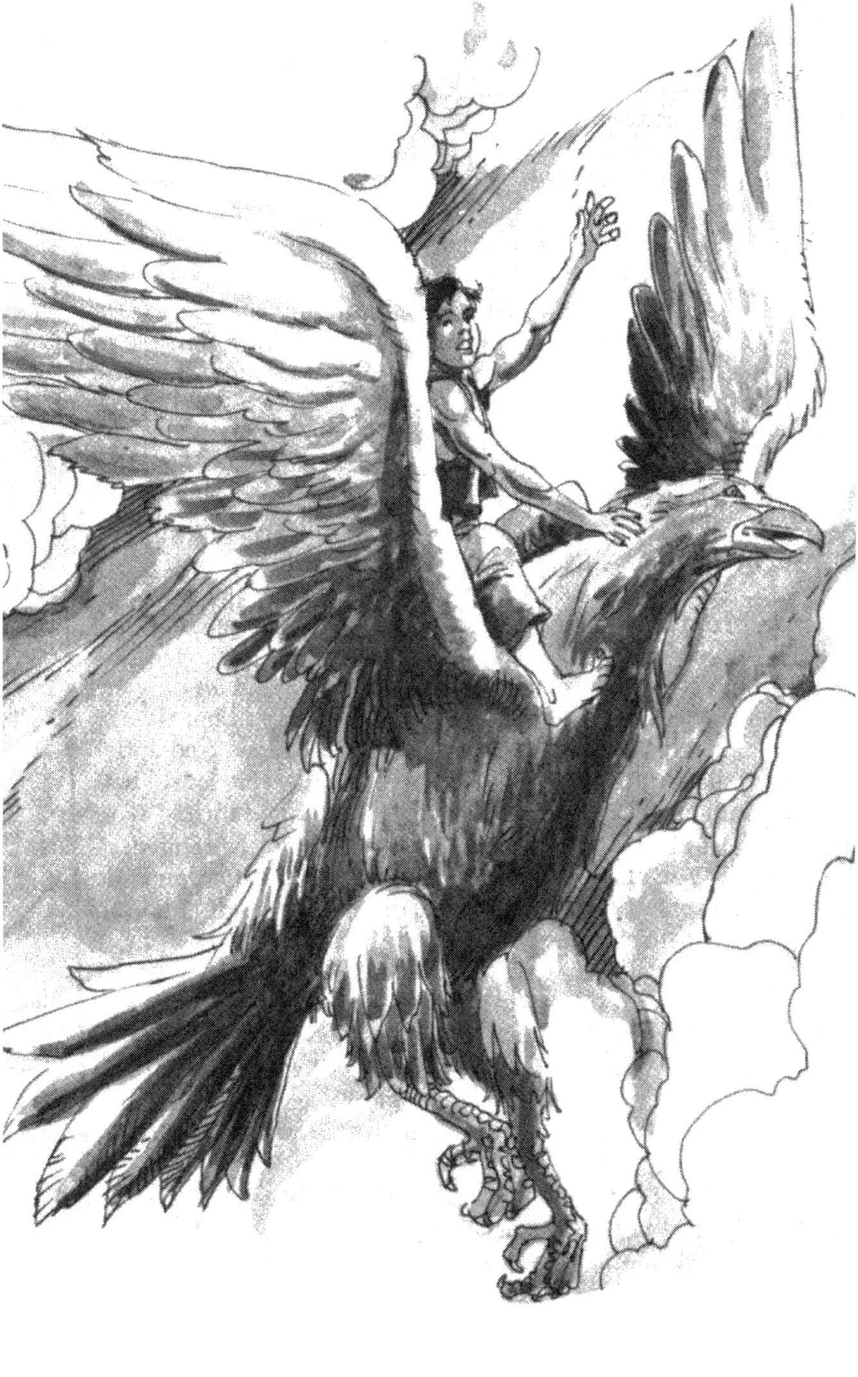

Magbaloto walked and wept some more, and at last he met the West Wind. Magbaloto told him his trouble and the West Wind said, "I do not know the way to heaven, but my friend the Eagle might. Walk on until you meet him."

So Magbaloto walked and wept some more until at last he met the Eagle.

"Why do you weep, Magbaloto?" the Eagle asked.

"Do not ask me why I weep unless you promise to help me," said Magbaloto.

"I do not see how I can promise if you do not tell me your trouble," said the Eagle.

Magbaloto told his story again, and when he had finished, the Eagle said:

"Get on my back and I will take you straight to heaven."

Magbaloto climbed on the Eagle's back and the Eagle spread his great wings and flew. They flew up, and up, and up until they reached the sky. There the Eagle rested on the top of a high mountain and said, "Get off now and seek her whom you love. I shall wait for you here."

Down the streets of the sky Magbaloto walked and walked until he came to Makaya's house. He found her with her grandmother, but when he begged the old woman to let him take Makaya to Earth with him, she replied:

"You shall not take my granddaughter from me unless you spread ten jars of sesame on the sand to dry and then gather them up again before nightfall."

With a heavy heart Magbaloto spread the sesame on the sand, and in the afternoon, as soon as they were dry, he started gathering them as fast as he could. He had gathered no more than a few handfuls, however, when the sun began to set. So he sat down and wept.

Along came the King of the Ants and asked, "Why do you weep, Son?"

"Ask not why I weep," replied Magbaloto, "unless you pledge to help me."

"How shall I help you unless you first tell me your trouble?" said the King of the Ants.

Tale of the 101 Brothers and Their Sister

The Wonderful Birth

LONG AGO there lived a poor couple. Fervently they begged Allah to give them children, but the years followed one another and no child came.

Finally the wife said to her husband, "I don't think there is such a thing as Allah."

"Of course there is no real Allah," replied the husband. "We have long asked Allah for children, and what has he given us? Only poverty and old age!"

But very early next morning the wife called to her husband, saying: "Husband, husband, come here this minute! I am having a baby!"

"What insanity has taken hold of you?" he said. "Only last night you were complaining that you were childless. Now you say you are having a baby!"

But the woman yelled for help so earnestly that the man went to her, and sure enough, she soon gave birth to a baby boy.

"This baby's birth is a miracle!" said the husband.

"What 'this baby's birth' are you talking about?" said his wife. "Help, for here comes another!" And this time she had a baby girl.

"Marvelous, marvelous!" the husband said. "Wife, you are really marvelous to give me twins—and at your age!"

"What 'twins' are you talking about?" she replied. "Help! Here's another coming!" And she bore a second baby boy.

This went on until, trying to catch his breath, the husband begged his wife:

"Enough, enough! I have lost count of our babies."

"All right then," she replied. "Now see how many there are in all."

With great difficulty the man counted the babies, and he found that his wife had given birth to 102 children, everyone of them a boy except one girl. Soon the babies started crying, and the man and his wife began to worry about how they were going to feed so many babies.

By and by the man picked up his kris. "I think," said he, "that we have too many babies. We must get rid of some of them."

"Stop!" the woman shouted. "Why kill them? Take them to the roadside. There people will pick them up and raise them."

"All right," said the man. He picked up five of the babies and carried them off. But he did not leave them at the roadside. He walked to the edge of an abyss and threw the babies in. Then he returned home, picked up the next five babies, and threw them into the abyss, too. He did with the rest of the babies what he had done with the first until only the girl remained. When he picked her up, too, his wife exclaimed:

"Don't throw the girl away! We must keep her."

But the man paid her no heed, and he threw the girl into the pit. When he looked into the bottom of the pit, however, he found everyone of the 102 children all alive and walking about. He was much surprised at this and he pitied them. He gathered 102 young fern leaves, all that he could afford to feed his children with. He dropped the leaves in the pit and walked home.

The children each took a fern leaf and ate it, and what do you think happened? The boys became handsome full-grown men, and the girl a most beautiful maiden. They looked as healthy as normal young people look, and in fact they were even more healthy than most people are, as you shall soon enough see.

Now, after all had eaten their fern leaves, the eldest of them turned to the others and said: "The first thing we must do is to get names for each of us. To begin, what name will you give me?"

"Rajah Bagaram!" the others said, and so Rajah Bagaram he was named.

Then to their only sister Rajah Bagaram gave the name Putri Intantiaya. To the boy after her he gave the name Maongagen, the Wise. The fourth child he named Barakat, the Miracle-Worker. Thus Rajah Bagaram gave each of his brothers the name to show what he would be good in doing.

Then Rajah Bagaram asked Pokakandak, the Maker of Arms: "Get me a kris."

Pokakandak prayed and soon a gold-plated kris appeared before them all. Next Rajah Bagaram asked the Geographer to tell them where there was land that would be suitable for them to live in; and the Geographer told him of a region seven hills away to the west, called Ingud a Bulawan, or Land of Gold.

Rajah Bagaram said that he would go to Ingud a Bulawan. He added that during his absence Maongagen, the Wise, should take charge of the family. Then he said: "If after a month I fail to come back, come and look for me."

The Monster

Next he asked Pamamana, the Archer, to shoot him to Ingud a Bulawa, the Land of Gold. This Pamamana did, and in a trice he reached the place. He found the land to be a land of great beauty, but it was strangely uninhabited. He walked about until he came to a palace, and inside that he found a golden bed. He sat on the edge of the bed wondering where the people had gone. By and by there entered a woman beautiful beyond description and with gold-tipped hair.

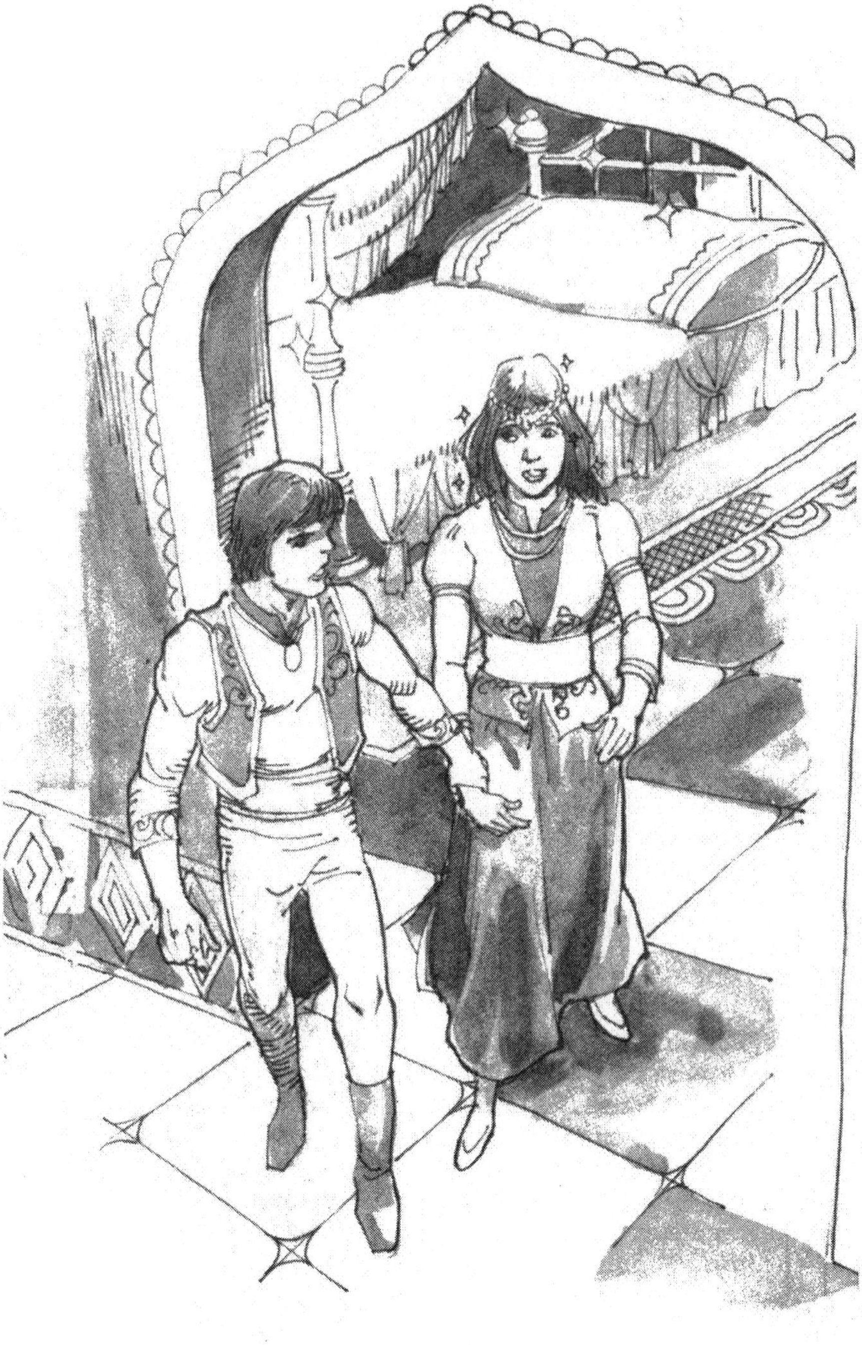

Rajah Bagaram told her his name and asked who she was. The maiden offered Rajah Bagaram a chew of betel nut as a sign of friendship. Then she said, "My name is Towan-Putri Malano-tiaya, daughter of the Sultan of Ingud a Bulawan."

"And are you all alone?" asked Rajah Bagaram.

"The other people of this unhappy land," she replied, "have been devoured by the Ta-awi. I beg you to leave before it is too late. I am his prisoner."

Rajah Bagaram refused to leave and promised to save her. While he was yet speaking, a loud noise was heard, and soon the Ta-awi, a monster most fearful to see, entered.

"Ah, this is good," said the Ta-awi. "I thought I would have nothing for supper, but here is a delicious-looking young man. And he is good-looking, too! I shall eat him before I go to bed," he added, turning to seize Rajah Bagaram. Instantly Rajah Bagaram pulled out his kris and thrust it into the monster, and it fell to the floor with a heavy thud.

While the Ta-awi lay dying, it disgorged a quantity of eyeballs. Rajah Bagaram and the princess knew that these eyeballs were those of the Ta-awi's many victims. They gathered the eyeballs and put them in a large jar.

Towan-Putri Malano-tiaya agreed to marry Rajah Bagaram and together they lived happily in the palace.

The Golden Hair in the Water

One morning soon after, the young couple went to bathe in the river and a strand of the princess's hair was carried off by the stream. Now the river ran through the Sultanate of Banjarmasir. It happened that while the hair was passing through Banjarmasir, the sultan's son, Sumusong sa Alongan, was bathing there. Towan-Putri Malano-tiaya's gold-tipped hair twined itself around his finger. The prince ran to his father with it and said:

"Father, you once told me never to marry anyone except a girl with gold-tipped hair. Why didn't you tell me that such a girl lived upstream?"

"How did you know such a girl lived there?" asked the sultan.

"Here is a strand of her hair. It was carried down by the stream while I bathed in it, and it got caught around my finger."

"Why, Son," said the sultan, greatly surprised, "I never knew such a girl lived anywhere in the world! I did not want you to marry, so I told you to marry only a girl who had gold-tipped hair. But now I will see what can be done to win her for you."

So saying, the sultan ordered seven of his most trusted men to find out where the girl with a gold-tipped hair lived.

The men followed the course of the river. They arrived at Ingud a Bulawan after passing seven hills and seven mountains. There they came to a palace where they found the beautiful woman of the gold-tipped hair, but they discovered that she was married. They returned home and told the sultan: "We have found her of the gold-tipped hair. She is beautiful beyond words and her hair is as lovely as her face. But she is married, and it will be necessary to steal her."

"You have done your job well," said the sultan and sent them away.

Then he ordered his poisoners to make a very deadly poison. They made a poison so strong that whoever looked at it would instantly die.

Back to Ingud a Bulawan went the seven trusted men with orders to poison the princess' husband and carry the princess back to Banjarmasir.

Meanwhile, Towan-Putri Malano-tiaya, while asleep, dreamed that seven men entered the palace, poisoned her husband, and carried her off. She rose greatly troubled and told Rajah Bagaram, her husband, about her dream. She was sore afraid and wrapped her husband in a long skirt, tied both ends of the skirt, and put the bundle in a room. Then she shut and barred the palace doors and waited.

By and by the seven men from Banjarmasir arrived. They tried to enter the palace but found all the doors barred. So they taunted Rajah Bagaram, saying:

"You cowardly prince! If you are not an effeminate datu, come out of your hiding place and fight!"

These words stung Rajah Bagaram's pride. He tore himself out of the skirt, grabbed his kris, and ran to meet those who had insulted him in his own house.

When he stepped out of the door, the men held up the poison before his eyes and he dropped down dead. Then they entered the palace, and against her violent protests they carried Towan-Putri Malano-tiaya off to Banjarmasir.

A month had passed, and Rajah Bagaram's brother and their sister asked Paririmar, the Diviner to find out what happened to their brother.

"He is dead," replied Paririmar.

"His body," added the Geographer, "lies in Ingud a Bulawan."

Then Maongagen, the Wise, asked Pamamana, the Archer, to send them all on his arrows to Ingud a Bulawan. This the Archer did, and at the palace they found Rajah Bagaram's body. Then Pangongoyag sa Miatay, the Reviver, restored him to life and Rajah Bagaram told them his strange adventures. The brothers were much angered to hear how he had been murdered and how his bride had been stolen. Maongagen asked Pamamana to send them all to Banjarmasir, leaving only the recuperating Rajah Bagaram and their sister.

The Flying Litter

Soon the ninety-nine brothers found themselves on the playgrounds of the Sultan of Banjarmasir. There the sultan's subjects were gathered to hear the sultan speak. The sultan told his people that he would give two-thirds of his kingdom to whoever could do two things: make the princess from Ingud a Bulawan speak and stop a mysterious fire from coming between her and his son whenever the latter tried to get near her.

But before proceeding with our story, we should tell that when Towan-Putri Malano-tiaya was brought to Banjarmasir, she was very much grieved over her husband's death. She wept day and night and refused to speak with anyone. And whenever Sumusong sa Alongan, the prince, tried to speak to her, a mysterious fire sprang up in full blaze between them. This was how things stood when the ninety-nine brothers appeared in Banjarmasir.

And now after the sultan had spoken, he asked the brothers to enter the palace where a war dance was going on. Pagsasayan, the Dancer, took part, and so well he danced that all the people clapped their hands and shouted their praises for him.

The applause made Towan-Putri Malano-tiaya look, and when she saw the strangers, she found how closely they resembled Rajah Bagaram. She then knew they were his kin, and she went to the sultan and said: "Uncle, let us give these strangers something to eat. Feeding strangers is one of the rules of hospitality."

The sultan heard her speak, was delighted, and ordered that food be served the ninety-nine strangers.

Then Sumusong sa Alongan, the sultan's son, tried to sit beside Towan-Putri Malano-tiaya, but instantly the mysterious fire blazed forth and stood between him and the princess.

So the sultan turned to Maongagen, the Wise, whom he saw was the leader of the strangers, and asked him: "When one of your men made the princess talk, you performed half of the job. Now stop the fire from appearing between her and my son, and as your reward I will give you two-thirds of my kingdom."

Maongagen went aside with three of his brothers—with Paririmar, the Diviner; with Barakat, the Worker of Miracles; and with Mabagur, the Strong. Then, having reached an agreement with them, he turned to the sultan and said: "Have a litter built that can hold a thousand people. Then on the litter let the groom and the bride, together with your seven most trusted men and your ten best poisoners, be carried around the palace three times. After that the wedding can proceed."

The sultan little suspected the plot and ordered a gigantic litter built. Then he had Sumusong sa Alongan and Towan-Putri Malano-tiaya carried aboard the litter. The seven men who had poisoned Rajah Bagaram and stolen Towan-Putri Malano-tiaya he also sent aboard, and after them the ten men whose poison had killed Rajah Bagaram. Finally the sultan ordered his strong men to lift the litter and carry it around the palace.

But Barakat, the Miracle-Worker, made the litter so heavy that the sultan's men could not lift it. Three hundred men, six hundred men, and finally a thousand of the sultan's strongest subjects tried to lift the litter together, but they failed to do so.

Then Maongagen asked the sultan to order his thousand litter-bearers to board the litter. All the men went aboard and Maongagen told Mabagur to lift it. Without difficulty Mabagur raised the litter, including all the people it contained, and the sultan danced with joy.

The sultan's joy, however, was short-lived. For instead of carrying the litter around the palace, Mabagur gave a sign to Barakat, the Miracle-Worker, who used his magic power to raise the litter to a height of ten rooftops from the ground and make the litter remain afloat there. As the litter rose, Mabagur clambered onto it and stood protectingly over Towan-Putri Malano-tiaya.

Then the sultan was seized with terror. "That's too high, that's too high!" he cried out. "Now bring down the litter and carry it around the palace so that my son may marry the princess."

But Maongagen turned to the sultan and said: "Sultan of Banjarmasir, it is now the time for speaking. First you must know that we the ninety-nine strangers are the brothers of the man you ordered poisoned. The murderers stole his wife to give her to your son—your son who was not man enough to fight for her himself. For these things you shall now pay."

Then Maongagen gave a sign to Mabagur, and from the litter Mabagur dropped the ten poisoners and the seven kidnapers. Next Mabagur threw out Sumusong sa Alongan, and the sultan wept bitterly to see his son die.

When Mabagur turned to throw out the litter-bearers, too, Maongagen took pity on them. He stopped Mabagur and asked Pamamana, the Archer, to shoot up all the brothers onto the litter. This he did, and to the accompaniment of sweet music played by the brothers, they floated to Ingud a Bulawan, taking captive the thousand men still aboard the litter.

Then, amidst great great rejoicing, Rajah Bagaram and the lovely Towan-Putri Malano-tiaya were reunited.

War and Peace

The Sultan of Banjarmasir, burning with a desire for revenge, gathered his remaining warriors and invaded Ingud a Bulawan. But Mabagur, the Strong, went on top of the mountains and dispersed the invaders by rolling down rocks and trees against them.

The sultan retreated, but after a few days he came back with a thousand ships. Then Pamiminta, the Kidnaper, sent the invading ships to the bottom of the sea. The sultan was captured, and begging that his son and his dead subjects be restored to life, he agreed to make his sultanate a part of Ingud a Bulawan. He also agreed to marry off to any of the brothers his daughter, Putri Tandiong-amas, whom he had sent to grow up in the island of Bairan.

When these terms had been arranged, Pokakandak, the Magician, brought Putri Tandiong-amas over from Bairan. She proved to be as beautiful as Towan-Putri Malano-tiaya, and Maongagen, the Wise, married her. Then Sumusong sa Alongan, along with his father's dead subjects, was restored to life by the combined powers of the Miracle-Worker, the Magician, and the Reviver; and Putri Intantiaya, the only sister of the 101 brothers, agreed to marry him.

Rajah Bagaram asked his brothers to restore to life the parents of Towan-Putri Malano-tiaya, and he asked that their subjects be restored to life, too. Again the Miracle-Worker, the Reviver, and the Magician worked together, and soon one by one the dead sultan, his wife, and their numerous followers came out of the jar in which had been stored the eyes disgorged by the Ta-awi upon his death.

Next Pamamana, the Archer, shot all of them back to the old hut in which they were born. Their parents could not believe their eyes. The couple were persuaded to go with them to Ingud a Bulawan, and there they were welcomed by Towan-Putri Malano-tiaya and her parents.

Then the ninety-nine unmarried brothers went out in search of their own wives; and considering their numbers and their power, you may be sure their search covered a very wide area.

One night Rajah Bagaram spoke to his father and mother, saying: "Do you still believe that there is no Allah?"

"Why do you ask such a question, Son?" they asked.

"You may remember that before we were born you said you did not believe in Allah."

"How did you come to know that?" asked they.

"I ought to know," answered Rajah Bagaram. "All of us—my hundred brothers, my sister, and I—came from Allah, who wanted to show you that He exists."

The Tale of Sog-sogot

LONG, LONG AGO, in a mountain village in Northern Luzon there lived a man named Sog-sogot. The men of the village were fond of going out to hunt deer and wild hogs, and one day Sog-sogot went with them. They entered the woods with their dogs and hunted long and patiently but found no game.

At last Sog-sogot grew weary with walking. He went off to an open space in the woods and sat down to rest. By and by the sky darkened and Sog-sogot looked up to see a giant bird swooping down toward him. It was a *ban-og*, and it was so gigantic that it covered the sun.

Sog-sogot ran toward the trees to hide, but the ban-og pounced on him and seized him in its powerful talons. Then it rose into the air and flew off with him.

So terrified was Sog-sogot that he did not know what to do. And there was not much he could do, for the bird had risen high up to the clouds. Sog-sogot knew that if he should loosen himself from the bird's grasp, he would fall to the ground and get killed.

The ban-og flew on and on until it came to a very large tree that stood taller than its neighbors. It circled once or twice and then alighted on the tree.

A large nest lay at the top of the tree and two baby ban-og sat in the nest. The mother ban-og dropped Sog-sogot in the nest and flew away.

Sog-sogot then knew that the ban-og had brought him there to feed him to its fledglings. As soon as the ban-og had flown away he sought a way to escape. But so high was the nest and so large the trunk of the tree that he could not climb down. There were no branches by which he might descend and no clinging vines which he might hold on to. So he hid in the nest.

Soon the fledglings in the nest awoke, opened their mouths, and cheeped for food. Sog-sogot had grown hungry, too, and peeping at the baby birds, he saw a deer and three pigs which the giant mother bird had killed and brought home to her babies. Sog-sogot cut off a leg of the deer and ate all he wanted. Then he fed the baby birds with the pigs and what remained of the deer.

After they had eaten, the fledglings closed their mouths and fell asleep. Then Sog-sogot hid under the nest and wondered how he might escape.

By and by the mother bird came home with more deer and wild pigs. It dropped them in the nest and flew away to hunt for more. He cut off part of the deer open and ate his dinner. Then he fed the baby ban-og, too, and when they fell asleep, he hid under the nest as before and went to sleep, too.

This went on for days and Sog-sogot had plenty of food to eat. Now and then it rained, and he would catch some of the rain in his hands and drink. When no rain fell he would drink the warm blood of the deer as he cut one up.

But as time went on, Sog-sogot grew more and more worried about his young wife. He knew that she was worried about him, too, and he did not know what to do.

Before long the baby birds opened their eyes. Feathers grew on their wings and bodies, and Sog-sogot knew that soon they would fly out of the nest. How was he ever to leave the nest himself?

Fortunately, the birds did not harm Sog-sogot. He had fed them so often that they must have thought he was one of them.

After a few more days, the young birds were walking about the nest and flapping their young wings. One day, as one of them sat at the edge of the nest gazing at the neighboring trees, Sog-sogot grabbed its leg and jumped out of the nest. The bird was thrown off balance and fell fluttering to the ground with Sog-sogot clinging to its leg.

When they reached the ground, Sog-sogot ran like mad and was soon safely hidden from view. Then he walked on, eating whatever food he found along the way, until he came to the woods at the outskirts of his native village. There he met his wife. She was leading their two pigs and their cow, but she did not look at him. She just walked along the road as if he were a stranger to her.

Sog-sogot called to her and said, "Wife, where are you going with our pigs and cow? I have come home!"

His wife did not stop or look at him. She just walked on as if she did not see or hear him. So he ran to her and said, "I am very sorry I was away so long. I was caught by a *ban-og*, and I managed to escape only now." Then he told her the rest of his story.

When he had related everything to her she shook her head sadly and said, "I am not your wife. I am the spirit of your wife, who died while you were gone. Go home to your village and let me go to mine."

Sog-sogot wept bitterly when he heard these words and asked, "And where is your new village?"

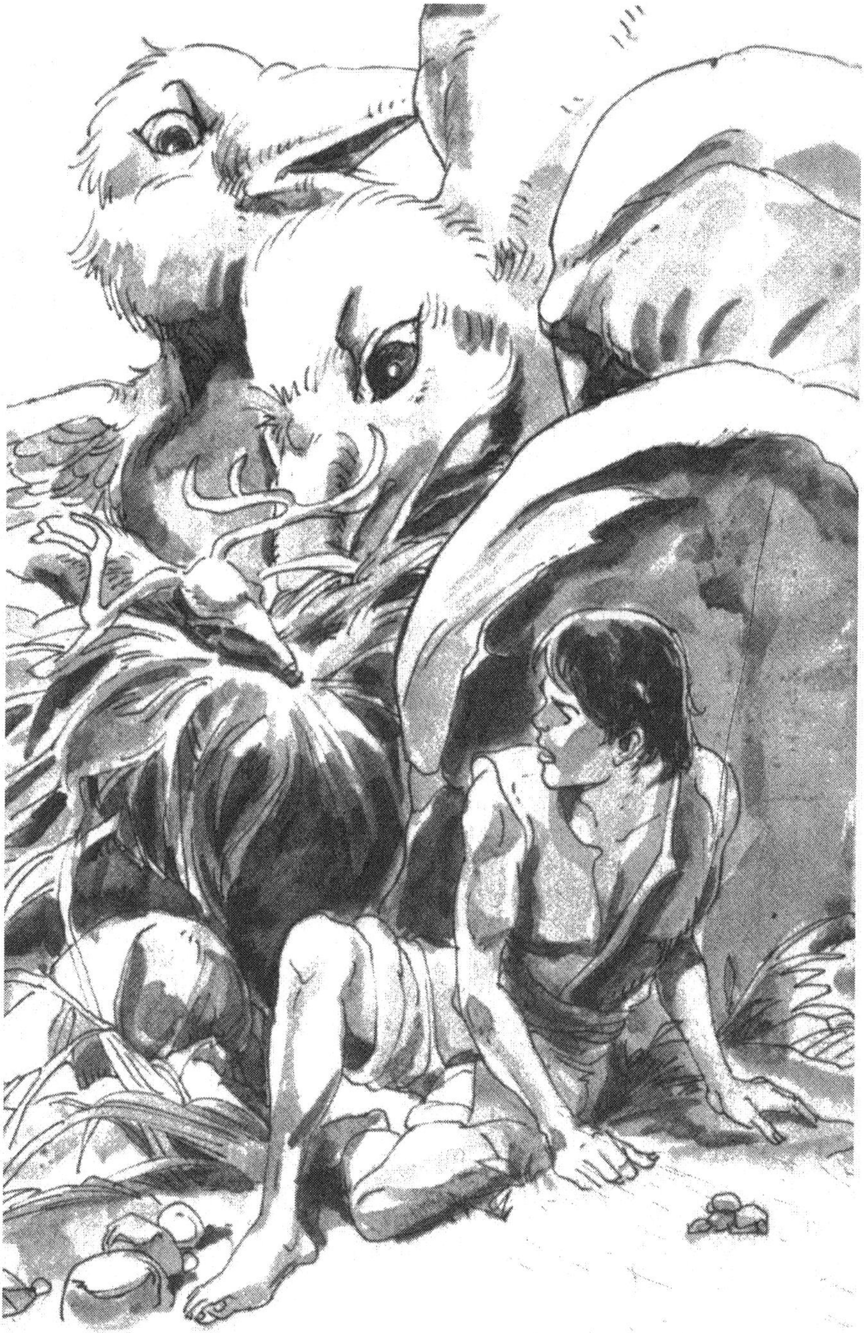

She pointed beyond the horizon and turned to go.

But Sog-sogot clung to her and said, "No, no! Do not leave me! I must go with you!"

But she walked on, saying:

"If you really want to come to the Spirit World with me, first go back to the old village and find a white chicken. The chicken must have white feathers, white legs, and a white beak. After you find one, bring it to me."

"How shall I know where to follow you?" said he.

"Follow the hoof prints of these pigs and this cow," she replied.

Sog-sogot hurried to the village and found the white chicken his wife wanted. He ran back and followed the hoof marks of the pigs and the cow until he came to a river where he found his wife bathing. "Here is the chicken you asked me to get," he told her.

She nodded and said, "I must go to the town of the spirits. If you really wish to come along, you may. But do not be afraid."

Sog-sogot promised not to be afraid and they rose to go. They walked on and on until they came to the town of the spirit-folk. They entered a house prepared for her, and she hid him with the white chicken in a rice bin inside the house. "Sit in this bin and keep still," she said. "When the spirits come to take you, pluck off some of the feathers of the chicken and throw them at the spirits."

Sog-sogot sat quietly in the rice bin and waited. Soon night fell and the spirits came into the house and said, "There is a living man here! We have come to eat him!" They searched every corner of the house and Sog-sogot plucked a few feathers from the chicken, his whole body trembling with fear.

When they opened the bin and tried to snatch him, he threw the feathers at them. They were so terrified at this that they ran away.

Sog-sogot spent the night and the next day in the bin. The next night the spirits came again. They entered the house and opened the bin but he dispersed them by throwing feathers at them.

For two weeks this went on, and as the days passed, the chicken feathers became fewer and fewer. Soon no more feathers remained, and Sog-sogot went to his wife and said, "The chicken feathers are all gone. I think I should leave your world and come back when it is time for me to die."

    She agreed and gave him some rice to eat on his way home. She showed him which way to go and said, "Go back to our people, and when your time to die comes, you need not bring a white chicken. You will not be eaten by the spirits, for you will be one of us."

    Sog-sogot bade his wife farewell and they parted.

    He walked back to his native village, and the people asked where he had been all this time. "Your wife is dead and your pigs and your cow are dead, too," they said.

    Hearing these words, Sog-sogot knew that she who had taken him to the Spirit-World was indeed the spirit of his wife. The people wondered greatly when he told them his adventures, and they gave offerings of delicious food to the good spirits for seeing him back home.

The Enchanted Snail

UPON A TIME there lived a childless couple. They often prayed to ask God to give them a child of their own, but none came. At last they prayed:

"O God, please give us a child, even if he be only like a snail."

Then, without warning, a baby was born to them. He was very tiny and resembled a snail so much that he came to be known as Snail. His parents loved him very much for all that. They kept him sheltered in the house fearing he might get lost if they let him play in the yard.

One day Snail went to his mother and said, "Please let me go and look for food. I am old enough to go out into the world."

His mother shook her head and said, "No, my son. You are very tiny and helpless. If you go out you might get lost or someone might step on you."

But Snail was insistent. "I am old enough to take care of myself, Mother," he said. "Please let me go."

She saw that her son could not be dissuaded and so she let him go. "Be very careful, Son, for you are very frail," were her parting words.

Snail headed directly for the river. There he saw some women fishing. They were putting the fish they caught in baskets they had placed on the grassy bank of the river.

Snail crept into the basket containing the most fish and

sat quietly there. By and by the owner of the basket came, picked up the basket, and started for home.

She had not walked far when Snail yelled with all his might: "Rain! Rain! Rain!"

"Now what's that?" thought the woman.

"Rain! Rain! Rain!" repeated Snail.

The woman became so frightened that she dropped the basket and ran home.

Then Snail climbed out of the basket and carried it home. "Here is food for you to cook, Mother," he said.

The mother opened the basket and found shrimps, crabs, and dalag in the basket. She boiled the fish with tomatoes and salt, and they had a fine dinner that day.

The following morning Snail went back to look for food. He met an old man carrying the head of a cow. The old man was walking away from the village and Snail patiently followed him.

Soon the man reached a friend's house. He hung the cow's head on a bamboo fence and entered the house to chat with his friend. Snail quietly climbed up the fence, crept into the cow's ear, and sat still.

Before long the old man came out and then took the cow's head and walked home. When he reached a lonely place, Snail cried out:

"Ai! Ai! Ai!"

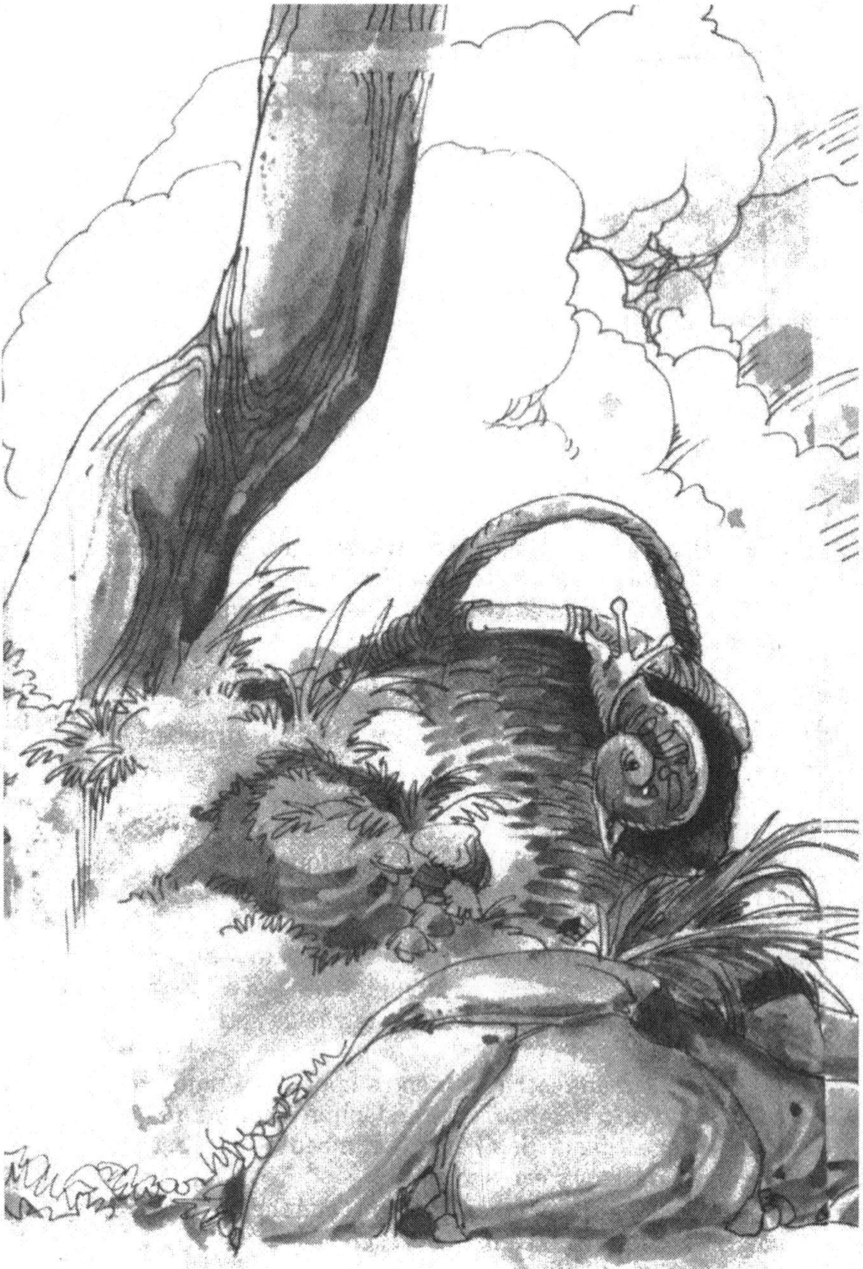

"What's that!" thought the old man.

"Ai! Ai! Ai!" Snail repeated.

The old man was so frightened that he dropped the cow's head and fled home. Then Snail got out and carried the cow's head to his mother.

After a few days Snail said, "Mother, I am in love with the chief's beautiful daughter. Please go and ask him to give her to me as my wife."

Snail's mother was greatly surprised at this request. "You are only a snail after all, my son," she said. "You must not expect me to be so bold as to ask the chief for his beautiful daughter's hand."

But Snail kept asking her to go until she finally went.

"Pardon me, O Chief," she said, "but Snail, my son, would like to marry your beautiful daughter."

The chief was amused at this request and said, "I shall ask my daughter, and if she will take a snail for her husband, he can have her." His daughter had refused many a handsome suitor before, and he felt sure she would laugh aloud when she heard the old woman's request.

But to his astonishment, his daughter, when she heard Snail's wish, smiled and said, "Thank you. I shall be very happy to take Snail for my dear husband."

"You must be beside yourself, Daughter!" the chief stormed. "How can you marry a mere snail?"

"He loves me and I love him. Isn't that enough?" she asked, for she had a strong will of her own.

So she and Snail were married, and the chief drove them out of the village as soon as the wedding ceremony was over.

The young couple lived in poverty far out in the fields. But at midnight on the seventh day, Snail, who at his birth had been enchanted by a witch, turned into a handsome young prince. His wife and his parents were very happy when they found this out. And upon hearing about it, the chief welcomed the young couple back into the village and treated them as his favorites.

The Man Who Tried to Cheat Death

WHILE EATING his dinner one day, a rich man heard his dog and his cat quarreling under the table. The man was surprised because he could understand their words clearly. "You eat too much," the cat was saying. "You should not eat everything placed before you."

"Our master gave us these scraps to eat," growled the dog. "Why should I not eat as much as I can?"

"If I were you," said the cat, "I would not eat so much."

"Why not?"

"Listen and I will tell you," said the cat. "Next week we shall have plenty of food to eat. All of our master's cattle will die, and there will be a lot to eat. Then if we are hungry, we shall enjoy our feast better."

"How do you know all this?"

"I just know," said the cat.

The man heard every word and thought out a plan to cheat Death. He did not want to lose his cattle without getting anything in return. So he drove his cattle to town and sold them all. "I am glad I learned what was about to happen," he thought, counting his money. "If I had not been warned I would have lost all my cattle."

From then on, whenever he was at the table, he listened closely to his dog and his cat.

Not long after this the man heard the cat say to the dog, "Why don't you leave some of the food for me? Our master gave the food for us to share with each other, and now you want to eat everything."

"I am very sorry," replied the dog, "but I have to eat all I can. Hard days are ahead for me. I will share you just enough food to satisfy your hunger."

"And you will eat all the rest?"

"Yes, but don't you worry," said the dog. "Tonight you will have all the food you want, and I shall have nothing."

"But if I will have food to eat, you will get some, too," said the cat. "I will give you plenty of food tonight if you are not too greedy now."

"There's no use," the dog replied. "I will have no time to eat tonight. I'll have a lot of work to do."

"Why?"

"Listen closely and I'll tell you," said the dog—and the man leaned down and listened closely, too. "Our poor master is going to die tonight," continued the dog. "His wife will cook plenty of food for those who will come and see his body. You will be under this table alone and eat all the scraps they throw to you. But I will be under the house keeping away the dogs who will try to steal the food."

When the dog had told his story, the cat said, "I am sorry for you, my dear friend. You may have all the food then."

The rich man heard every word and smiled to himself. "I am glad I learned about my fate," he said. "Last time, when I heard that my cows and carabaos were going to die, I sold them ahead of time and cheated Death. Now I will cheat Death too."

So saying, he went to a wise man and told him his story. "Tell me what I should do to cheat Death," said he.

The wise man shook his head sadly. "My son," he said, "I am very sorry, but you will have to die."

"I came to find out how I may cheat Death. I must cheat Death as I cheated him when he wanted to get my cattle."

The wise man shook his head again. "That was a big mistake," he said. "You should not have sold your cattle. You should have allowed Death to get them."

"But I did not want Death to get my property," said the other man. "If they had died, I would have nothing now."

"I know, but you were wrong to try to cheat Death," said the wise man. "If you had not sold your cattle, Death would have been satisfied with them. Death would not have come back for a long time. Now Death will return and get you."

"Can't you do anything for me? Can't I give Death money? Can't I give Death all the money I got for the cattle?"

"No," said the wise man. "I am sorry but that would not help you."

So the rich man left weeping. He went home to pray God that Death spare him. He promised to distribute his lands among the poor and to give his money to the church. "I am willing to live the life of a poor man if I can live longer," said he.

But when night fell, he grew weaker and weaker, and finally he lay down, and his wife wept over him.

Death had come for the rich man.

The Tale of Diwata

Diwata Turns into a Log

A LONG TIME AGO, in a faraway land there lived a prince named Diwata. He was at his prayers one morning when he beheld a vision of Inigambar, a maiden known far and wide for her great beauty. She was so lovely that Diwata fell in love with her and vowed to go and find her no matter where she might be.

With the help of his two younger brothers he built a big boat and loaded it with provisions for a long voyage.

Then they put out to sea, and for many days and nights they sailed over the water.

Diwata felt sleepy one morning and said, "I want to go to sleep. If anything unusual happens, be sure to wake me up."

His brothers promised to do so and steered the boat while Diwata lay asleep.

Day followed night and night followed day, but Diwata slept on, and his brothers wondered what strange sleep had taken hold of him.

Then they saw the sky darken. They knew that a typhoon was coming, and they tried to wake Diwata up. They splashed water on his face and stood him on his feet, but Diwata remained asleep.

Then the typhoon fell upon the boat in all its fury and the vessel broke to pieces. The two brothers were washed upon the shore of a wild, uninhabited island, and nothing more was heard of them.

Still fast asleep, Diwata floated this way and that, unmindful of what happened. Time passed and seaweeds and shells grew on his body. His skin hardened, too, and after some years he looked like a log floating about on the sea. Finally, in a storm, he was washed ashore.

A man and his wife went out fishing in the sea one day and came upon Diwata's body. "This log will be good for firewood when it is dried," said the husband and pulled it home, little knowing what the log really was.

"Let us leave it in the yard to dry," said his wife, and so they did.

A few days later the husband took his axe and went down to chip off some firewood from the log. When he struck the log, "Wife!" he exclaimed. "Come here quick. This log bleeds!"

"Don't be silly," replied his wife.

But when she looked, she found the log bleeding indeed.

"Let's not cut it," said the man. "Let's scrub off the weeds and dirt and see what it is."

No sooner said than done. They brushed off the seaweeds and shells that covered the log, and lo! up stood a handsome young man.

Of course the couple were very much surprised at this. They asked Diwata to tell them how it happened that he became a log, and Diwata told them he had fallen asleep on a boat but did not know what happened after that.

"Be our son, for we are childless," said the couple.

Diwata thanked them and said he would be very happy to be their son.

Diwata Seeks Inigambar

One day Diwata was walking in the woods when he heard a great commotion. He asked what the noise was about and was told that the Sultan's lovely daughter, Inigambar, who had been missing for many years, was being sought in the woods by the sultan's men.

Diwata wondered if this could be the same beautiful young woman whose image he had seen in his vision back in his native land. He asked his foster parents to let him go and look for her, but they shook their heads. "You might meet with some misadventure," said they.

But Diwata pleaded so earnestly that they let him go.

Diwata did not follow the old paths through the forest. He wandered through the pathless jungle until at last, weary from travel, he reached the foot of a tall mountain. He climbed the mountain and after a difficult climb reached its summit. There he found no grass or tree. He only found bones scattered about.

"This must be the home of a monster," he told himself. He looked cautiously about and found a cave. He entered the cave and came upon a magnificent dwelling. Walking in, he saw a beautiful table of solid gold. A golden chair stood on one side of the table and a silver chair on the other. He sat down on one of the chairs, and to his surprise two betel-nut boxes—one of gold and the other of silver—floated into the hall and placed themselves on the table. Diwata understood this to be a sign of welcome, so he took some betel nut and chewed it.

Looking around, he saw an inner room. He entered and found a maiden sound asleep. He walked softly to

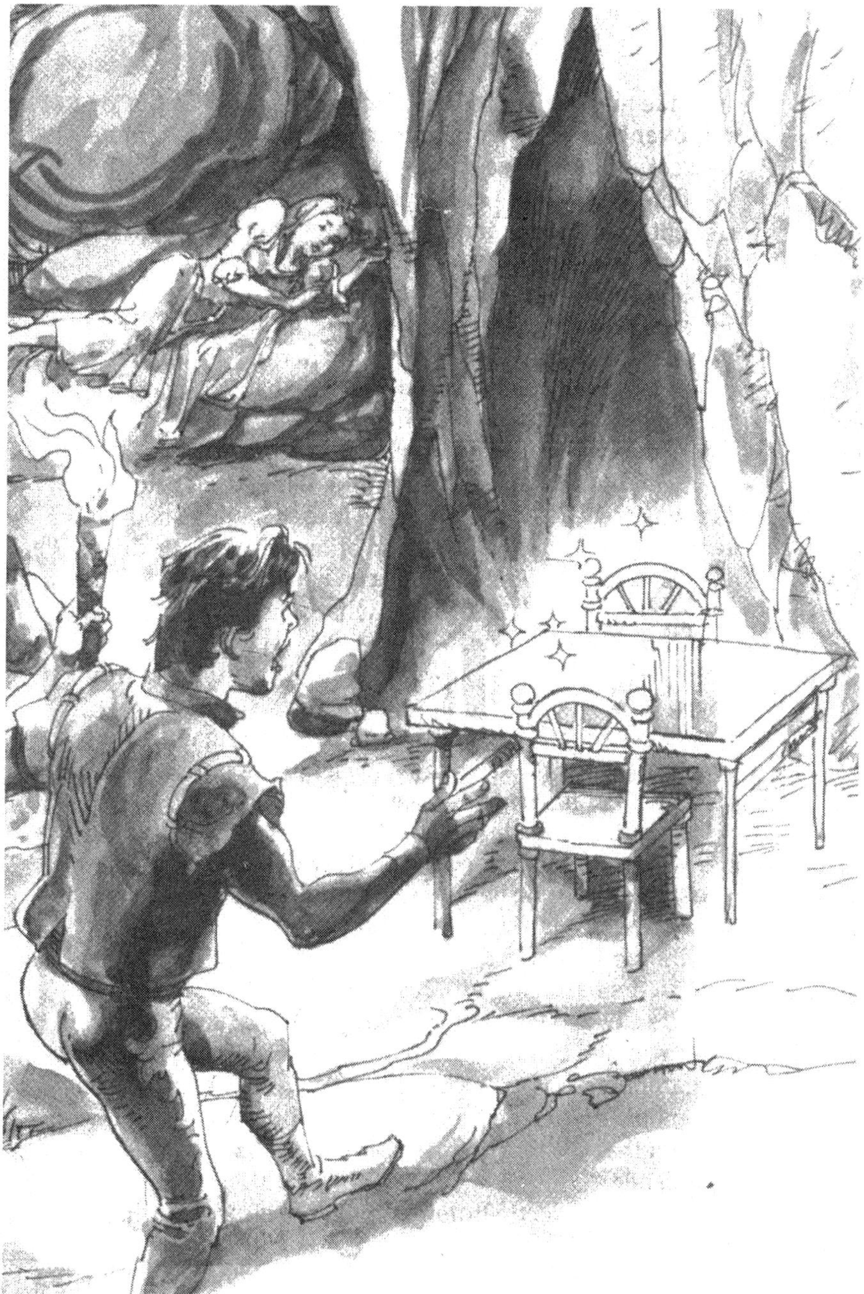

her side and looked into her face, and great was his joy to discover that she was Inigambar, the woman whom he had come so far to seek.

Before long she woke up. She saw him and was delighted. "At last my prayers have been answered!" she said. "My deliverer has come."

She explained that she had prayed earnestly and long for one to come and rescue her. In turn he told her that it was at his prayers that he first saw her in a vision.

"Then the Lord must have willed that you come and deliver me," she said.

"From whom shall I deliver you?" asked Diwata.

"Have you not heard about the winged monster Garuda?" she asked. "When he flies, his wings sound like ten thunderstorms. The sweep of his wings pulls down houses and uproots trees. He can carry six men in his talons, and I shudder to think what will happen if he finds you here."

Even as he spoke, Diwata heard a fearful noise from the distance.

"That's the Garuda now!" exclaimed Inigambar. "I must save you!" So saying, she used her magic power and transformed him into a louse and hid him in her hair.

Soon the Garuda entered, and the floor shook under his weight. He dropped to the floor the bodies of several beasts and men he had brought home. "Where are you, girl?" he thundered.

Inigambar tried to be as calm as she could and met him in the hall. But with his keen scent, the Garuda detected Diwata. "I smell a man!" he said, sniffing about.

"You just brought in some dead men, Father," said Inigambar. "It is they you smell. What living man would be so bold as to enter your palace? Your power is so well known that the world does not mention your name above a whisper."

"It is so indeed. But now I want to clean your hair," said the Garuda.

This frightened Inigambar but she did not show her fright. "First let me go in my room and undo my hair-knot, Father," she said. She hastened into her room, hid Diwata beneath one of her fingernails, and loosened her hair. Then she went back into the hall.

The monster searched Inigambar's hair, sniffing suspiciously all the time. But he found nothing there, so he said at last: "You have no lice in your hair, I see. So now," he added, "I shall pare your nails."

"Just a moment, Father," said Inigambar. "I must first go in and comb my hair and tie it neatly into a knot." She hastened into her room, put the louse back in her hair, tied her hair into a knot, and returned to the Garuda.

The monster cut her nails, distrustfully peering underneath each nail. He found nothing there, and so at last he sat down to dinner.

After his meal the Garuda set out to hunt again, and Inigambar transformed Diwata into his human shape. Then Diwata whispered something in Inigambar's ear. To this she nodded her head, and they spoke nothing more about the matter till afterward.

Before the Garuda returned home again, Inigambar changed Diwata back into a louse and hid him in her hair. Then the Garuda arrived, dropped five more men's bodies to the floor, and said:

"Where are you, Girl?"

"Here, Father," said Inigambar, promptly coming out and laying his food on the table. She stood by him while he ate and said, "Father, I have now lived in your house many years. At first I was afraid of you, and there was a time when I even hated you. But now I know you better, and my fear and hatred are gone. I have learned to love you as if you were my own father."

The Garuda felt flattered when he heard these words. "Say more," he said.

"Now that I have learned to love you," she continued, "I wish you would help me keep you from harm. Tell me what objects can harm you so that I shall be careful to keep them from your enemies."

"Not one of my enemies will ever come here and live!" said the Garuda.

"That is true, but men are crafty where they lack strength," replied she. "It is strange because I am a man's daughter, but I love you as my own father now that I know you better."

"I am glad to hear that," said the Garuda. "Now," he added, "only two things can do me harm. Both of these are hidden safely in my room."

"And these are?"

"One is an arrow and the other is a bottle. If the arrow is broken, my arms will break, too. If the bottle is shattered, I will lose my life. But as I said before, none of my enemies will ever touch them and live."

"I will guard the arrow and the bottle just the same," she said.

Inigambar Tricks the Garuda

Early next day when the Garuda was about to go out hunting, Inigambar asked him, "Father, when will you return home? Can you not hunt a little longer so that you need not go out often? I hate to be left alone so frequently."

"I shall be out hunting for seven days this time," said the Garuda and left.

Then Inigambar used her magic power, changed Diwata back into his human form, and told him about the Garuda's secret. They entered the Garuda's room and found large stores of gold, silver, and precious stones piled up in a corner. But they did not mind these treasures. They only took the arrow and the bottle and hurried away—but not before Inigambar had told her comb, her powder, and her rouge to answer the Garuda for her if the monster spoke to her.

Meanwhile, the Garuda thought about the strange questions Inigambar had asked him. He regretted that he had told her his secrets and decided to make sure that she was not planning mischief. So he hurried home, dropped his usual catch to the floor, and called out, "Where are you, Girl?"

"I will come out in just a moment, Father," replied Inigambar's comb. "I will just arrange my hair."

The Garuda waited, but as Inigambar did not appear, he said, "Well, come now, Girl!"

In turn Inigambar's powder replied, "Only a moment more, Father. I will just powder my face."

The Garuda waited again but Inigambar did not come out, and he grew impatient. "Come now and lay my dinner on the table!" he thundered.

"In a moment, Father," replied Inigambar's rouge. "I'll just redden my lips first."

After another impatient wait, the Garuda strode into Inigambar's room. Then he found that Inigambar was not there and that her comb, her powder, and her rouge had been speaking for her. He searched the cave, and when he did not find Inigambar, his rage knew no bounds. Swiftly he transformed his arms into wings, flew out through the door, and soared up into the sky.

Before long he saw Inigambar and Diwata running to the edge of the mountain. He swooped down, and the lovers heard the noise of his powerful wings. They saw the earth darken as the monster's wings covered the sun, and they continued running way.

But the Garuda was soon overhead and roared, "Diwata, you are a pitiful man! Not only have you invaded my kingdom but you have stolen my daughter, too. Breathe your last, and prepare to die!"

So saying, he swooped down on Diwata.

Then Diwata pulled out the arrow and broke it on his knee, and the Garuda dropped to the ground with broken wings.

"Inigambar has told him my secret!" exclaimed the Garuda. "She must have given him the bottle, too!" So saying, he rose to his feet. He wanted to overtake them and crush them to death before they could break the bottle. But it was too late. Diwata smashed the bottle against a rock, and the Garuda fell down in a heap, dead.

Then Diwata and Inigambar left. After a long journey through the wilderness they reached Inigambar's native land. She told her overjoyed people how the Garuda had imprisoned her and how Diwata had finally rescued her.

Diwata and Inigambar were married amidst much rejoicing. Then Diwata and some of the people went back to the Garuda's cave. There they gathered all the gold, silver, and jewelry the monster had stolen and hoarded.

When the sultan grew old, he asked Diwata and Inigambar to rule the land after him, and they reigned happily and long, a delight to all the people.

Printed in Poland
by Amazon Fulfillment
Poland Sp. z o.o., Wrocław